BRISTOL

Travel Guide 2025

*Discover the Best of Bristol –
Attractions, Culture, Local Gems &
Practical Tips for an Unforgettable Trip*

ABIGAIL I ANDREA

Copyright

*All rights reserved.
No portion of this publication may be copied, shared, stored, or transmitted in any form—whether by electronic, mechanical, photocopying, recording, or any other means—without the express prior written consent of the copyright holder. Unauthorized use or duplication is strictly prohibited*

ABIGAIL I ANDREA

Table of Contents

Copyright 1
Table of Contents 2
Foreword 4
Welcome to Bristol 5
Bristol at a Glance 12
Top Must-See Attractions 20
Hidden Gems & Local Secrets 28
Experience Bristol Like a Local 35
Sample Itineraries for Every Traveler 43
Getting Around the City 52
Where to Stay in Bristol 60
Eat, Drink & Be Merry 69
Cultural Etiquette & Local Manners 77
Money Matters & Budget Tips 84
Packing Smart for Bristol 92
Staying Safe & Healthy 100
Responsible & Sustainable Travel in Bristol . 108
Bristol Month-by-Month 116
Language Tips & Local Lingo 126
For Every Type of Traveler 134
Maps, Visual Highlights & Quick Reference . 142
Final Notes, Challenges & Memories 150

Foreword

There's a unique magic that draws people to Bristol — a city where history and innovation dance together along winding streets, colorful harbors, and vibrant neighborhoods. My first visit here was unplanned, a spontaneous weekend getaway during a chilly spring, and yet it quickly became one of those trips that lingers long after the plane has landed back home. I remember wandering through the harbourside at dusk, the sky painted with soft oranges and purples, and catching the distant sound of street musicians mingling with laughter from nearby cafés. It felt alive, warm, and full of stories waiting to be discovered.

Bristol is a city that rewards curiosity. It's not just the iconic landmarks — the Clifton Suspension Bridge or the historic SS Great Britain — but also the hidden murals in Stokes Croft, the indie markets filled with local crafts, and the community spirit that pulses through every corner. It's a place where tradition meets creativity, where you can savor the finest local foods one moment and lose yourself in cutting-edge art the next.

This travel guide is born from a deep love of Bristol and a desire to share everything that makes this city so captivating. Whether you're here for a day or a week, an adventure solo or a family trip, you'll find stories, tips, and insights designed to help you connect with Bristol beyond the usual tourist trail. Expect practical advice, heartfelt recommendations, and a genuine invitation to experience the city as locals do.

As you turn these pages, I hope you'll discover the same joy and inspiration that I found — the feeling of stepping into a city that welcomes you like an old friend, with surprises at every turn and memories that will stay with you long after you leave.

Welcome to Bristol — your unforgettable adventure starts here.

Welcome to Bristol

Welcome to Bristol, a city that isn't just visited — it's experienced. Tucked along the River Avon in the southwest of England, Bristol has a way of greeting you with a wink. It's cheeky, creative, and colorful — a city that proudly wears its history on one sleeve and a spray-painted Banksy mural on the other.

This isn't a place where you merely tick off landmarks. Bristol invites you to wander through cobbled streets, sip cider with locals on a sunlit harbourside, and lose track of time browsing record stores, street food stalls, and vintage boutiques. And in 2025, the city is more alive than ever — eco-forward, culturally buzzing, and delightfully welcoming.

So, whether you're here for the street art, the maritime history, the indie vibes, or just a good old-fashioned adventure, you're in the right place.

A City with Deep Roots and Fresh Branches

Bristol's story is as layered as its Georgian townhouses and medieval cathedrals. Founded around a thousand years ago, the city flourished as a port — a major player in trade and, unfortunately, the transatlantic slave trade, which Bristol has since acknowledged and engaged with through art, education, and public discourse. Today, the city leans into its complicated past while shaping a progressive and inclusive future.

In 2025, Bristol is a hub for green innovation, community-driven arts, and music that spills out from every corner — from harbourside jazz nights to underground drum-and-bass events in converted warehouses. It's this unique blend of history and hipness that makes Bristol such a joy to explore.

First Impressions: What You'll See, Hear, and Feel

Arriving in Bristol often begins at **Bristol Temple Meads**, the city's historic railway station, designed by Isambard Kingdom Brunel himself. The station's Gothic arches feel like a time portal, and once you step outside, Bristol's energy hits you: street performers playing violins or beatboxing on Broadmead, students zipping past on bikes, buskers under the fairy lights of St. Nick's Market, and the gentle hum of conversation from riverside pubs.

You'll notice that Bristol is hilly — gloriously so. Walking from the harbourside to Clifton will give your legs a workout and reward you with sweeping views from **Clifton Suspension Bridge,** a marvel that spans the Avon Gorge with elegance. But it's not all postcard views. Every street corner holds a surprise: a bold mural, a tucked-away garden, or a café that feels like your new favourite hangout.

The Heartbeats of Bristol: Its Neighbourhoods

Bristol isn't a city with a single centre — it's a patchwork of unique, vibrant neighbourhoods, each with its own personality.

Clifton is all charm and class. Think leafy avenues, whitewashed terraces, and cafes where locals chat over artisan pastries. Don't miss a walk down the **Clifton Arcade**, an architectural gem filled with quirky shops and antiques.

Stokes Croft is Bristol's rebellious spirit personified. It's the city's unofficial graffiti gallery, with every building adorned in paint, protest, and poetry. Here, independent cafes like The Canteen serve live music with your vegan curry, and art collectives spill onto the streets.

Southville and Bedminster are where the city's creative side really kicks in. Converted warehouses now house galleries, studios, and co-working spaces. The **Upfest Gallery** here keeps the spirit of Europe's largest street art festival alive all year round.

Harbourside has transformed from an industrial zone to a culture-rich playground. You'll find everything from paddleboarders on the water to exhibitions inside **M Shed** and **We The Curious** — Bristol's science and discovery centre, now fully revamped in 2025 with a brand-new interactive sustainability wing.

Let the Locals Lead the Way

Bristol isn't flashy — it doesn't need to be. Locals are relaxed but passionate, and conversations come easy. Chat with a street vendor about where to get the best Sunday roast, or ask a cyclist at Queen Square for a scenic bike route. You'll get more than just directions — you'll get stories.

Travel tip: **Say "cheers" instead of thank you,** especially when someone pours you a pint or hands you a takeaway. And if someone calls you "my lover," don't blush — it's just a friendly West Country greeting.

Eco-Minded and Proud

You'll quickly notice how green-minded Bristol is. The city became the **UK's first European Green Capital** in 2015, and in 2025, it's leading the way in sustainable urban living. Electric buses, abundant bike lanes, rooftop gardens, zero-waste cafes, and refill stations are now standard city features.

Local businesses embrace slow fashion, conscious food sourcing, and circular economy practices. Take a stroll down **Gloucester Road,** said to be Europe's longest stretch of independent shops, and you'll find everything from refillable shampoo stations to hand-sewn vegan leather goods.

Seasonal Magic in the Air

There's no wrong time to visit Bristol.
* In **spring**, the **Ashton Court Estate** bursts into colour, and daffodils carpet the Downs.

* **Summer** means floating bars and pop-up cinema nights in Castle Park.
* **Autumn** is for cozy cafes and hot chocolate after a walk along the harbourside.
* And **winter** brings twinkling lights, Christmas markets in Millennium Square, and the beloved **Bristol Light Festival**.

Pro tip: Pack layers and **always bring a rain jacket** — Bristol weather changes its mind often.

Our Promise to You: This Is Your Bristol

This travel guide was written not just to help you plan a visit, but to help you feel the rhythm of the city before you even step onto its streets. You'll find useful details in the chapters ahead — tips on transport, hidden gems, food to obsess over, itineraries to follow (or break), and moments to remember.

But most importantly, you'll find **Bristol as it is today: bold, bohemian, thoughtful, and full of life.**

So welcome, traveler. Explore with open eyes, listen closely to the stories in its stones and songs, and fall into step with a city that will surprise you again and again.

Bristol's got a seat saved just for you. Let's get started.

Bristol at a Glance

Compact yet cosmopolitan, historic yet forward-thinking — Bristol is the kind of place that defies a single definition. Located in the heart of the South West of England, this city of just under half a million people has grown from a medieval trading port to one of the UK's most dynamic urban destinations. It's a city of contrasts that harmonize: 18th-century townhouses sit beside avant-garde murals, and traditional Sunday roasts share menus with vegan jackfruit tacos.

Before you dive into its colourful streets and cultural nooks, let's take a moment to get a broad, meaningful sense of what Bristol is all about in 2025.

Where Is Bristol and Why Does It Matter?

Geographically, Bristol lies about 120 miles west of London and 80 miles south of Birmingham. The city stretches along the **River Avon**, with the **Severn Estuary** flowing out toward Wales, which is just a short train ride away. Its riverside location gave rise to its early prosperity, making Bristol one of the most significant ports in England from the 12th century through the 19th.

Today, Bristol is a bridge between worlds — a gateway to the lush countryside of **Somerset and Gloucestershire**, while remaining firmly in the pulse of modern innovation. It's a launching pad for adventures, but also a destination in its own right, laced with charm and depth.

A Brief but Mighty History

Bristol's story is long, textured, and often sobering. It was a powerhouse of shipbuilding and overseas trade, and sadly, it also played a central role in the transatlantic slave trade — a dark chapter the city continues to confront through public art, museum exhibitions, and education.

In recent decades, Bristol has emerged as a socially conscious and self-reflective city. From **Colston's statue being removed in 2020** to continued dialogues around inclusivity and reparative justice, the city has embraced its past while striving to shape a better future.

This sense of civic engagement is part of what makes Bristol so compelling — its people are passionate, its streets speak volumes, and its art is as political as it is beautiful.

Bristol by the Numbers (2025 Edition)

* **Population:** Approx. 470,000
* **Climate:** Temperate oceanic — mild winters, cool summers, unpredictable rain (always carry a brolly!)
* **Currency:** Pound Sterling (£)
* **Time Zone:** GMT / BST (in summer)
* **Dial Code:** +44
* **Public Transport:** First Bus Network, West of England Metrobus, and a growing electric bike-share program
* **Official Language:** English
* **Local Government:** Bristol City Council (with a strong push towards green policies and inclusive development)

Neighbourhoods That Define the City

Understanding Bristol starts with exploring its diverse neighbourhoods, each like a piece of the city's character puzzle.

Clifton: Elegance and Elevation

This picturesque district is home to some of the city's oldest architecture, leafy walks, and of course, the iconic **Clifton Suspension Bridge**. The area is brimming with boutiques, cozy cafés, and stunning views of the Avon Gorge.

Stokes Croft: Art's Wild Heart
You don't just visit Stokes Croft — you feel it. It's the unofficial graffiti capital of the UK and home to an anarchic, creative spirit. Here, art is activism, and walls talk — often loudly.

Southville and Bedminster: Creative Soul
Once industrial quarters, these areas have transformed into some of the trendiest spots in Bristol. Expect pop-up galleries, vegan bakeries, and thriving weekend markets like **Tobacco Factory Market**.

Harbourside: Waterfront Wonder
A walk along the revamped harbour area offers floating bars, art installations, and museums like **We The Curious** and **M Shed**. It's a beautiful blend of history and modernity, ideal for a sunset stroll or paddleboard session.

Easton: Multicultural Mosaic
Known for its diversity and vibrant street scenes, Easton is Bristol's heart of global

cuisine and community activism. Colourful houses and community gardens speak to a neighbourhood that's proudly inclusive.

A Taste of Local Culture

If you want to understand the rhythm of Bristol, start with its sound. Music is embedded into the city's DNA — it birthed trip-hop in the '90s with artists like **Massive Attack** and **Portishead**, and its underground music scene is still pulsing with bass and innovation. You'll find live music in pubs, converted churches, and even on boat stages moored in the harbour.

Street art is another cultural pillar. **Banksy**, perhaps the world's most famous street artist, began here. His early works are still visible around the city (ask locals — they know where to look), and they've inspired generations of muralists who continue to decorate Bristol's walls with wit and power.

Cider is practically a religion here, with the **Bristol Cider Shop** and local favourites like **The Apple** serving up varieties you won't find anywhere else. But if hops are your thing, the local craft beer scene has exploded in 2025 with breweries like **Left Handed Giant**,

Wiper and True, and **Good Chemistry Brewing** leading the charge.

Modern Bristol: Green, Smart, and Forward-Thinking

Bristol isn't just playing catch-up in sustainability — it's setting the pace. As of 2025, over 40% of the city's buses are electric, and there are dozens of car-free zones introduced under the new **Bristol Clean Air Plan**. Rooftop solar panels, urban gardens, and co-living spaces are becoming the norm.

The city also prides itself on being a leader in social enterprise and ethical business. Many of its independent shops and restaurants are co-operatives or locally owned, and sustainable fashion is just as common as vintage wear. Bristol's ethos is simple: **Live local, buy local, think global.**

When to Visit and What to Expect

Bristol has something special to offer every season.

* **Spring (March–May):** Cherry blossoms in parks like **Queen Square**, outdoor terraces come alive, and the **Bristol Walk Fest** invites you to explore the city on foot.

* **Summer (June–August):** Festival season! Don't miss the **Bristol Harbour Festival**, **St Pauls Carnival**, or **Balloon Fiesta**. Long evenings and buzzing energy abound.

* **Autumn (September–November):** A quieter charm settles in. Leafy walks on **The Downs** and crisp cider tastings are the order of the day.

* **Winter (December–February):** Twinkling lights, Christmas markets, and theatre shows fill the dark with cheer. The **Bristol Light Festival** in early February adds a magical glow.

A City That's Easy to Explore, Hard to Leave

Thanks to its compact size and efficient public transport, you'll never be far from your next discovery in Bristol. Walking and cycling are often the best ways to explore, especially if you want to linger at independent shops, snap photos of hidden murals, or simply follow your curiosity down a narrow alleyway.

If you're staying for a weekend or a full fortnight, Bristol has the rare gift of adapting to your pace — it can be leisurely or lively, modern or historical, quirky or quiet. It's not a city that is overwhelming. Instead, it unfolds gently, inviting you in with every new corner turned.

Top Must-See Attractions

Bristol doesn't wait for you to discover it — it introduces itself boldly and unapologetically. From soaring bridges and steampunk ships to hands-on science centres and open-air galleries, the city's attractions don't just sit quietly behind velvet ropes. They invite you to climb, touch, taste, wander, and wonder.

Whether you're a history lover, an art chaser, a culture seeker, or simply someone who wants to feel the pulse of a place through its most cherished sights, Bristol in 2025 is brimming with top-tier experiences. Let's dive into the can't-miss landmarks and attractions that will make your Bristol trip unforgettable.

Clifton Suspension Bridge: The Icon of the Avon

Let's start with the showstopper. The **Clifton Suspension Bridge** isn't just an architectural marvel — it's Bristol's most photographed symbol. Designed by engineering legend Isambard Kingdom Brunel (though completed after his death), this 1864 structure stretches elegantly across the **Avon Gorge**, offering panoramic views that make even the locals stop and stare.

By 2025, the bridge now features an upgraded visitor centre, with interactive displays explaining not just its daring design, but the social and political challenges faced during its construction. For the most breathtaking view, head there at golden hour when the setting sun lights up the cliffs and the river below glows like molten copper.

Travel Tip: Walk across the bridge from the Clifton side at dusk, then stop at **The White Lion Bar** for a drink on the terrace — you'll get one of the best rooftop views in the city.

SS Great Britain: Step Aboard Living History

All aboard! The **SS Great Britain** is far more than just a ship — it's a floating time machine. Built in 1843 and also designed by Brunel, this was the world's first great ocean liner. Now permanently docked in Bristol's **Great Western Dockyard**, it has been lovingly restored into a museum experience like no other.

You'll wander through the first-class cabins, peer into cramped steerage quarters, and even smell the coal, tar, and gunpowder of the engine room (yes, really — the scent is piped in for authenticity!). As of 2025, the new "**Voices from the Voyage**" exhibit uses AI-powered projections to let passengers from history tell their tales.

Don't Miss: The "invisible glass" dry dock viewing chamber where you can walk beneath the hull — a surreal and slightly eerie glimpse at the giant iron belly that once ruled the seas.

We The Curious: Science, Art, and Curiosity Collide

Refreshed and reinvigorated after its full redevelopment, **We The Curious** is Bristol's interactive science and culture centre, re-opened in 2024 with a bold new vision: "**Everyone's a Scientist**." This is where kids and adults alike can conduct experiments, write messages in light, float giant bubbles, and question how the universe works — all under one futuristic roof.

The **Planetarium** here is a highlight, with 360° digital shows that now include live, real-time satellite feeds from space. In 2025, they've also added a new sustainability lab, powered entirely by solar energy, where visitors can explore the future of climate tech and biodiversity.

Fun Fact: On weekends, local artists and musicians often collaborate with scientists to host immersive experiences — imagine learning about black holes while surrounded by ambient live music and projections!

Bristol Cathedral: Tranquil Beauty in the City Centre

If you're craving a peaceful pause, step into **Bristol Cathedral** — a Gothic masterpiece tucked beside College Green. Its soaring vaulted ceilings, kaleidoscopic stained glass, and centuries-old tombs create an atmosphere of quiet awe. The cathedral's history dates back to 1140, yet in 2025, it continues to evolve, with art installations and music performances adding a contemporary layer to its sacred space.

Stroll through the adjoining gardens, where stone benches and blooming borders offer the perfect moment of reflection amid the city's buzz.

M Shed: Bristol's Story, Told by Its People

Forget stuffy museums — **M Shed** tells Bristol's story in a way that feels intimate, emotional, and surprisingly alive. Located on the harbourside, this free museum focuses on the **people of Bristol**, past and present, with powerful exhibitions on activism, migration, trade, and local legends.

The top floor offers unbeatable views over the harbour, while the restored industrial cranes outside still rumble into life on special weekends — a nod to Bristol's days as a port city.

Local Highlight: Check out the "**Protest & Power**" exhibit launched in 2025, featuring multimedia displays of Bristol's activism, from the suffragettes to the toppling of Colston's statue and beyond.

St Nicholas Market: A Feast for the Senses

Hungry? Head straight to **St Nick's Market**, a covered arcade brimming with mouth-watering street food, quirky craft stalls, and some of the best independent vendors in the city. Smell the Ethiopian coffee from **Full Court Press**, taste handmade samosas from **Matina**, and browse through rare vinyl or retro treasures at the pop-up stalls.

As you eat your way through the global street food aisle, you'll hear street musicians, chat with passionate stallholders, and likely fall in love with something handmade you didn't know you needed.

Pro Tip: Visit on a Wednesday or Friday when the outdoor **Street Food Market** expands into Corn Street.

The Bristol Museum & Art Gallery: Artifacts and Imagination

Perched near the university, the **Bristol Museum & Art Gallery** is a majestic Edwardian building with a dazzling collection inside. From ancient Egyptian mummies to wildlife dioramas and fine art by Turner and the Pre-Raphaelites, it's a deep and varied dive into global and local history.

In 2025, they unveiled the **"Bristol Reimagined"** digital art installation — a room where historical paintings are reinterpreted using AI animation, giving visitors a unique window into how the past might have felt in motion.

Ashton Court Estate: Where the Wild Meets the City

Just a 20-minute walk from Clifton, the sprawling **Ashton Court Estate** feels like a slice of the countryside brought right to the city's edge. Deer roam freely through ancient woodlands, mountain bikers race through designated trails, and kite-flyers dot the hills on breezy days.

It's also the launchpad for the **Bristol International Balloon Fiesta** every August — a jaw-dropping event where over 100 hot air balloons drift into the skies, drawing spectators from around the world.

The Banksy Trail: Art That Talks Back

No visit to Bristol is complete without spotting a **Banksy**. The elusive street artist got his start here, and you can still find several of his original works hidden across the city — from "The Mild Mild West" in Stokes Croft to "Well Hung Lover" near Park Street.

For 2025, local creatives have launched the **Banksy Audio Walk**, a self-guided app tour that combines GPS triggers with stories, interpretations, and even interviews from local residents about how the art has shaped their city.

A City that's Alive in Every Corner

While these are Bristol's headline acts, they're only the beginning. The real magic lies in the moments between: wandering past a mural you didn't expect, hearing music float down from a rooftop, tasting something new at a street corner you'll never forget.

The attractions may draw you in — but it's the spirit of the city that'll stay with you.

Hidden Gems & Local Secrets

Bristol is a city that rewards those who look twice. Beyond the big-ticket landmarks and postcard-perfect attractions lies a second city — a more intimate, layered version that pulses with local pride, eccentric charm, and unexpected magic.

This chapter is for the curious traveler. The one who takes the long way, peeks down side streets, chats with baristas, and follows the scent of bread or music wherever it leads. Bristol's hidden gems are less about ticking boxes and more about moments — moments that surprise you, connect you, and make you feel like you've unlocked something special.

Ready to wander off the well-trodden path?

The Christmas Steps Arts Quarter: History, Art & Tea-Lit Magic

Tucked quietly off the bustling city centre, the **Christmas Steps** is a crooked, cobbled alleyway so quaint it feels like a movie set. But what many visitors miss is what it leads to — the **Christmas Steps Arts Quarter**, a micro-neighbourhood bursting with creativity and old-world charm.

Boutiques here sell handmade jewellery, alternative comics, and offbeat vintage clothing. **That Thing**, a locally-loved shop, stocks fashion pieces from Bristol's own designers. Stop by **Chance & Counters**, a board game café where you can sip craft beer while playing retro and modern tabletop games.

At night, the steps glow with warm fairy lights, and a soft hush falls over the area — it's one of the few places in the city that still feels untouched by time.

Local Tip: Visit during the quarterly **Christmas Steps Night Market**, when artists spill out onto the street and live jazz drifts from basement bars.

Snuff Mills: The Secret Woodland Escape

While many visitors stroll the famous Downs or Ashton Court, few venture into **Snuff Mills**, a serene woodland tucked along the River Frome in northeast Bristol. Once the site of an old tobacco mill (hence the name), this hidden haven now offers tranquil walks, stone bridges, and moss-covered ruins that feel like a portal to another era.

It's a favorite of early morning joggers, dog walkers, and in-the-know locals seeking a breath of peace. You'll spot herons, dippers, and even the occasional otter if you're patient.

Explorative Suggestion: Follow the riverside path upstream to **Oldbury Court Estate**, where open fields and picnic spots await — a perfect place for a lazy afternoon.

Redcliffe Caves: The Underground Mystery

Beneath the city's surface lies a labyrinth of hand-dug tunnels known as the **Redcliffe Caves**. While rarely open to the public, occasional tours and events grant you access to these sandstone passageways that were once used for storing wine and even holding prisoners of war.

In 2025, Bristol's alternative theatre group **Kilter Theatre** has launched a new immersive experience down here — part history tour, part performance art. With only lanterns lighting the way, and echoing footsteps around every bend, this is one of the most unique and atmospheric adventures in town.

Note: Tickets sell out fast — sign up for early release alerts on local event platforms like Headfirst Bristol.

Totterdown's Painted Streets and Skyline Views

South of the River Avon, the hillside neighborhood of **Totterdown** is often overlooked in favor of more central districts. But this is a mistake you won't want to make. Known for its rainbow-colored houses that climb the steep roads like a box of crayons, Totterdown is a hub for local artists, families, and free spirits.

Walk the steep streets — yes, it's a workout — and you'll be rewarded with some of the best panoramic views of the city. Small cafes like **Fox & West** serve up excellent coffee and cakes, and hidden parks such as **Perrett's Park** offer an unbeatable sunrise perch.

Bonus: The **Totterdown Front Room Arts Trail** in November transforms the neighborhood into an open house of creativity, with painters, potters, and performers welcoming you into their homes and studios.

St. Werburghs City Farm: A Rural Patch in the Urban Tangle

Imagine goats grazing beneath a graffiti-covered railway arch, and you've got the delightful paradox that is **St. Werburghs City Farm**. Nestled in a quirky, eco-conscious part of town, this urban farm is free to visit and beloved by children and grownups alike.

Next door is **The Farm Pub**, a rustic community space built with reclaimed timber, where the garden hosts weekly live music, food pop-ups, and spoken word sessions.

Sustainability Note: In 2025, the farm has added a new "Edible Education" garden and runs zero-waste workshops throughout the year. This is the kind of place where you can both pet a pig and learn how to ferment your own kimchi.

The Lanes of Old Market: Queer Culture, Vintage Cool, and Vegan Eats

Old Market is Bristol's edgy heart — a revitalized area where LGBTQ+ venues, record stores, and eccentric tailors all share the same few streets. Once a slightly forgotten zone, it's now become a home for creative entrepreneurs and the queer community.

Check out **Old Market Assembly**, a buzzing venue with live music, wood-fired pizza, and one of the most inclusive vibes in the city. Just around the corner, **Glitch Studio** is a digital art gallery showcasing cutting-edge work from emerging local artists.

Curious Fact: Bristol was the first UK city to elect an openly gay Lord Mayor — and Old Market's transformation is deeply entwined with its history of resistance and community.

Secret Street Art in Stokes Croft and Beyond

While most tourists spot the obvious Banksy pieces, real street art hunters head to **Stokes Croft** and **Montpelier** for the raw, living gallery of Bristol's soul. Here, entire buildings are murals, alleyways bloom with political graffiti, and local legends are immortalized in color.

In 2025, the **People's Republic of Stokes Croft** collective continues to curate community murals, some of which respond directly to global news and local activism. Street art here isn't decoration — it's dialogue.

Tip: Join a **street art storytelling tour** led by artists themselves. You'll not only learn the meaning behind the work but hear about the city's radical history from those who paint it.

A City Best Discovered Through Whispers and Wandering

The best way to uncover Bristol's hidden gems? Ask a local. Sit down at a pub and chat with the person beside you. Linger in the charity bookshops of Gloucester Road. Follow your nose toward fresh bread baking or distant drums beating. This is a city where the unexpected often turns out to be the most memorable.

Hidden gems aren't always on the map. But in Bristol, they're never far away.

Experience Bristol Like a Local

There's a particular moment when you realize you're not just visiting Bristol — you're *feeling* it. Maybe it's when you find yourself dancing to a reggae DJ in a tiny bar hidden behind a curtain, or when you're chatting about politics and pastries with a barista who remembers your name. It's not just about seeing landmarks or sampling restaurants. It's about rhythm. Pace. Vibe. Energy.

To truly experience Bristol like a local in 2025, you'll need to let go of the itinerary now and then. You'll need to say yes to weird events, walk without a map, and trust that the city will show you what it wants you to see. Because behind every colorful mural, bustling cafe, and side-street gig is a story — and Bristol loves storytellers.

Let me take you by the hand and show you how we live here.

Start Your Morning with Slow Coffee and Big Conversations

In Bristol, coffee is a ritual, not a rush. Forget chain stores — this city runs on independent cafes that double as community hubs.

Locals begin their day at spots like **Small Street Espresso** in the Old City, or **Little Victories** in Wapping Wharf. These places don't just serve expertly poured flat whites and flaky almond croissants — they serve a slice of the city's soul. Expect baristas who remember your name and ask what you're working on. Expect to overhear passionate debates about housing reform or upcoming art installations.

If you really want to blend in, order something seasonal (like a locally foraged herbal infusion), grab a seat by the window, and take your time. In Bristol, lingering is encouraged.

Stroll the Harbourside Like It's a Sunday, Even If It's Tuesday

There's something meditative about walking Bristol's harbourside. The boats bobbing gently. Cyclists weaving through cobbled paths. Musicians busking outside M Shed. Even on weekdays, you'll see locals taking breaks to soak in the rhythm of the water.

For the full experience, start at **Spike Island**, a contemporary art gallery housed in a former dockside warehouse. Chat with the artists-in-residence, then wander along the water past **Underfall Yard**, where maritime history comes to life.

Don't miss **Cargo** — a series of repurposed shipping containers that now house tiny eateries, bakeries, and local craft shops. Grab a bite from **BOX-E,** a small restaurant run by a husband-and-wife duo, or try **Salt & Malt** for sustainably caught fish and triple-cooked chips eaten with a view.

Here, life slows down. You're not in a hurry — you're in Bristol.

Eat Like a Bristolian: Casual, Creative, and Community-Driven

Ask any local and they'll tell you — Bristol's food scene in 2025 is less about Michelin stars and more about **mission**. Restaurants here are an extension of values: local sourcing, sustainability, inclusion. And there's no better place to experience that than **Easton**.

This diverse, multicultural neighborhood has long been the heart of Bristol's global food scene. Take a lunchtime stroll down **Stapleton Road** and you'll pass Syrian bakeries, Jamaican grills, Indian curry houses, and Somali cafes. One favorite? **Somali Kitchen,** a cozy spot with spiced lamb wraps and the kind of warm hospitality that makes you feel like family.

Want something more grassroots? Attend a **pay-what-you-can supper club** — locals host rotating dinners in community halls or even their own homes. You'll sit at long tables with strangers and share a meal that nourishes more than just your stomach.

Dive into Bristol's Music — But Not Where You Think

Yes, Bristol birthed trip-hop giants like Massive Attack and Portishead. But the heartbeat of the city's music scene today lives in pubs, warehouses, and record shops.

Skip the tourist-packed bars and find your way to **The Crofters Rights** in Stokes Croft. It's part dive bar, part microbrewery, and part underground music venue. Or head to **The Jam Jar**, a DIY space in Lawrence Hill that hosts everything from Balkan folk nights to Afrobeat dance parties.

Record culture is alive and thriving too. Dig through crates at **Idle Hands** (specializing in dubstep, grime, and UK techno) or spend hours at **Wanted Records**, where staff will happily recommend vinyl that suits your mood.

Want to go full local? Attend **Trinity Centre's Community Open Mic** — a joyous, raucous event where anyone with a song or poem is welcome.

Shop Sustainably and Second-Hand — Because That's the Bristol Way

Bristol is proudly green, and locals wear that badge on their recycled denim sleeves. Fast fashion is frowned upon. Vintage, upcycled, and artisan-made are the default.

If you're after one-of-a-kind finds, head to **Gloucester Road** — the UK's longest stretch of independent shops. Here, every storefront tells a story. **That Thing** stocks quirky fashion from local designers. **RePsycho** offers upcycled 70s gear. And **Wild Oats** is where eco-conscious Bristolians stock up on bulk grains, handmade soaps, and plastic-free products.

Even better? Many stores now host workshops. Make your own body butter, sew your own patches, or bind your own journal. In Bristol, shopping is an act of participation.

Live the Pub Culture — But Go Off-Script

To really experience Bristol like a local, you must spend at least one lazy afternoon in a proper pub. But not just any pub.

Avoid the big chains and stumble into places like **The Coronation Tap** in Clifton — famous for its dangerously strong Exhibition cider and lively banter. Or **The Old Bookshop** in Bedminster, where jazz bands play between bookshelves and the food menu is constantly reinventing itself.

And if you want to see the true local spirit? Visit **The Star & Garte**r in Montpelier. Once a legendary reggae pub, it's been revitalized by the community and remains a temple to good music, strong drinks, and Bristol's proud Afro-Caribbean heritage.

Unwind the Bristolian Way: Wild Swims and Secret Gardens

Yes, locals love a good dip — even in chilly waters. **Cleeve Bay** and **Henleaze Lake** are secret spots where Bristolians gather for sunrise swims or post-work plunges. Pack a thermos of tea and join them. There's something bonding about braving cold water together.

If swimming isn't your thing, seek out the city's quieter green spaces. While Ashton Court and The Downs are popular, **Royate Hill Nature Reserve** offers woodland paths, foraging opportunities, and even the occasional pop-up forest yoga class.

Experiencing Bristol like a local isn't about knowing every street name or finding the "cool" places. It's about connection — with people, with places, with the pulse of a city that invites you to slow down, speak up, and stay curious.

Talk to the muralist painting a wall in the rain. Buy bread from a baker who still mills her own flour. Join a protest. Attend a drumming circle. Visit a zine fair.

Because once you do, you won't just *visit* Bristol.
You'll belong to it — even if only for a while.

Sample Itineraries for Every Traveler

Bristol is not a one-size-fits-all destination. It's a patchwork of culture, creativity, and contradictions — just waiting to be stitched into your own personal adventure. Whether you're a history buff, foodie, family traveler, or someone who just wants to wander, Bristol has something tailored for your taste.

In this chapter, I've curated a range of thoughtful, flexible itineraries that reflect how locals and travelers truly experience the city in 2025. You'll find real rhythm here — not a rigid schedule, but a helpful outline to inspire your own Bristol story.

Let's dive into five distinct itineraries, each offering a different lens on this colorful, welcoming city.

1. The First-Timer's Whirlwind (2 Days)

Perfect for: Those who want a bit of everything, fast.

Day 1: Classic Sights & Harbourside Vibes

* **Morning:** Start at **Bristol Cathedral**, with its gothic arches and serene cloisters. From there, stroll through **College Green**, past the old University buildings that anchor the city's historic core.

* **Midday:** Walk down Park Street, browsing indie shops, before heading to **M Shed** — a free museum that tells Bristol's story through art, objects, and voices.

* **Afternoon:** Grab lunch at **Wapping Wharf** (I recommend **Pizzarova** or **Cargo Cantina)** and then take a ferry ride across the harbor.

* **Evening:** Watch the sunset at **Clifton Suspension Bridge**, then settle in at **The White Lion Bar** for a pint with a view.

Day 2: Street Art, Ships & Local Flavors
* **Morning:** Head to **Stokes Croft** for a graffiti walk — this is Banksy's hometown, after all. You'll spot murals, political slogans, and street performers everywhere.
* **Midday:** Explore **SS Great Britain**, Brunel's engineering marvel — step inside this restored Victorian ship for an immersive maritime experience.
* **Afternoon:** Treat yourself to a classic cream tea at **The Ivy Clifton Brasserie** or a cheeky cider at **The Apple**, a boat-turned-bar moored in the harbor.
* **Evening :** Catch live music at **Thekla**, another boat venue, or **The Fleece** for that true Bristol gig scene experience.

2. The Art Lover's Escape (3 Days)

Perfect for: Creative souls and visual storytellers.

Day 1: Street Art & Independent Galleries

* Start in **Stokes Croft** and **Montpelier**, neighborhoods pulsing with murals and grassroots art.

* Visit **The People's Republic of Stokes Croft Gallery,** and don't miss **The Bristol Zine Library**.
* Lunch at **Canteen**, where rotating exhibitions often decorate the walls.
* In the afternoon, take a guided **street art tour** — many are hosted by former graffiti artists and offer insider perspectives.
* Dinner at **Souk Kitchen** in Southville, an artsy neighborhood rich in creative spirit.

Day 2: Contemporary Meets Classic
* Explore **Arnolfini** by the harborside — a contemporary art gallery hosting bold and often provocative exhibitions.
* Stroll over to **Spike Island**, where artists work on-site in open studios.
* Stop for lunch at the on-site café and strike up a conversation with a local printmaker.
* In the evening, attend a performance or spoken word event at **Watershed** or **The Wardrobe Theatre**.

Day 3: Photographic Moments & Cultural Memory
* Morning visit to **Royal West of England Academy (RWA)** for sculpture, painting, and photography in a grand Victorian setting.

* Walk to **Brandon Hill Park**, home to **Cabot Tower**. Climb up for breathtaking panoramic photos of the city skyline.
* Unwind with a sketchbook in **Queen Square,** a leafy Georgian square beloved by artists.

3. Family Fun in the City (3 Days)
Perfect for: Parents, grandparents, and curious kids alike.

Day 1: Hands-On History & Playful Discoveries

* Begin at **We The Curious**, Bristol's incredible interactive science museum (reopening in 2025 after major upgrades!).
* Visit the **Planetarium**, where star shows delight kids and adults alike.
* Afternoon stroll to **M Shed,** where little ones can climb into cranes and explore vintage buses.
* End the day with fish and chips at **Salt & Malt**.

Day 2: Animals, Boats & Balloons
* Catch the ferry to **Bristol Zoo Project**— a conservation-led space with spacious habitats and a focus on endangered species.

* Picnic in the surrounding **Wild Place Project** fields.
* On return, stop at **Ashton Court Estate** to see the deer park or rent bikes for family trails.
* Evening option: Take a hot air balloon ride with **Bristol Balloons** (age restrictions apply), a memory your kids will never forget.

Day 3: Treasure Hunts & Story Time
* Discover **The Georgian House Museum**, which offers scavenger hunts and costumed guides.
* Visit **St. Nicholas Market** for quirky souvenirs, then reward the kids with ice cream from **Swoon**.
* For some downtime, head to **Windmill Hill City Farm**, where children can meet animals, plant herbs, and play freely.

4. The Eco-Conscious Explorer (2 Days)

Perfect for: Green travelers who care about sustainability and local impact.

Day 1: Conscious Cafés & Ethical Markets

* Start your day with a zero-waste breakfast at **Koocha Mezze Bar** — plant-based Persian dishes served with sustainability in mind.
* Wander **Gloucester Road**, Europe's longest strip of independent shops — brings a tote for vintage finds and locally made goods.
* Lunch at **Café Kino**, a vegan co-op that often hosts activism events.
* Spend the afternoon at **St. Werburghs City Farm**, where you can volunteer or just soak in the green goodness.
* Dinner at **Root**, where vegetables are the star and waste is minimal.

Day 2: Green Spaces & Wild Walks
* Walk the **Bristol Green Capital Trail**, which winds through parks, permaculture gardens, and eco-initiatives.
* Visit **Arnos Vale Cemetery** — part historic site, part nature reserve, and one of Bristol's most peaceful places.
* Cap off your day with drinks at **The Lazy Dog**, an eco-conscious pub with community values and organic ales.

5. The Slow Wanderer (1 Day or Forever)

Perfect for: Travelers who don't want to rush.

If you're the kind of person who prefers one great conversation over five monuments, this one's for you.

* Start with **coffee and a book** at **Storysmith**, a local independent bookshop with a cozy reading nook and specialty brews.
* Walk aimlessly through **Totterdown**, the colorful hillside neighborhood known for steep streets and spontaneous art.
* Chat with artisans at **The Tobacco Factory Market** — you might end up buying a handmade journal or signing up for a pottery class.
* Eat lunch at **Café Grounded**, where locals read poetry between bites.
* Spend your afternoon on a bench by the **Floating Harbour**, watching the city drift by.
* No need for a plan. Bristol loves a wanderer.

The best Bristol trip is the one that feels like yours. These itineraries are starting points, but don't be afraid to stray. Bristol rewards curiosity and spontaneity. Strike up a chat with a stranger, follow the sound of drumming down a side street, or spend a little too long in that one record store you stumbled upon.

This isn't just a city. It's a living story. You're invited to write your own chapter.

Getting Around the City

Bristol may seem sprawling at first glance — its hills, harborside sprawl, and distinct neighborhoods can give the impression of a much larger metropolis. But once you start exploring, you'll find that Bristol is incredibly accessible, and its pace feels more like a big village than a big city. Whether you're navigating the cobbled Old City, crossing the Avon on a ferry, or cycling along leafy paths, getting around is part of the adventure.

In this chapter, we'll walk you through all the ways to travel smoothly, sustainably, and stress-free through Bristol in 2025 — whether you're here for a weekend or a month. The good news? You don't need a car. The better news? You'll see more, meet more people, and enjoy Bristol's rhythm better without one.

Walking: The Best Way to Feel the City

Bristol is a walker's city. Its central districts — like Clifton, Harbourside, the Old City, and Stokes Croft — are compact and best explored on foot. In fact, walking often ends up being faster than driving or taking public transport, especially during peak hours when Bristol's narrow roads can become congested.

Wander down **Park Street**, with its quirky shops and steep slope, or meander along the **Floating Harbour**, where boats bob beside you as you stroll past galleries and street performers. Historic **Christmas Steps**, cobbled and atmospheric, leads you from the Centre up into one of the city's oldest quarters — a walk worth taking slowly.

Local Tip: Wear comfortable shoes. Some areas, like Totterdown and Brandon Hill, can be steep, and Bristol's famous ups and downs will give your calves a workout.

Buses: Reliable and Expanding in 2025

Bristol's bus network, operated primarily by **First Bus**, has seen real improvements in recent years. In 2025, real-time tracking apps, greener hybrid fleets, and expanded service on popular routes will make the bus system more efficient and eco-friendly.

You can now tap your contactless card or smartphone to board — no need to fuss with exact change. Fares are capped daily and weekly, so even if you take multiple rides, you won't be charged more than the maximum limit.

Key Routes to Know:
* **The Metrobus (m1, m2, m3):** Rapid transit buses with dedicated lanes, perfect for getting to major points like the **City Centre, UWE (University of the West of England), Cribbs Causeway**, and **Ashton Vale**.
* **Service 8/9:** Circles through Clifton, the zoo, and Bristol University — great for sightseeing.
* **Airport Flyer A1:** Connects the city centre with **Bristol Airport** in about 30 minutes.

Apps to Download:
* **First Bus App** – for route planning, live updates, and digital tickets.
* **Travelwest Journey Planner** – excellent for combining bus, train, walking, and cycling options.

Cycling: Join the Two-Wheel Revolution

Bristol wears its cycling crown proudly. As one of the UK's first "Cycling Cities," it continues to invest in bike infrastructure — from separated bike lanes and lock-up points to e-bike hire hubs.

The 2025 rollout of **YoBike+**, Bristol's smart dockless electric bike-sharing program, has made cycling even more accessible. With a simple QR code scan, you can hop on a bike, ride across town, and leave it at any designated zone.

Popular Routes:
* **The Bristol-Bath Railway Path:** A scenic, 13-mile trail on a former train line, perfect for leisurely rides.
* **Harbourside Loop:** Flat, well-paved, and visually stunning — ideal for beginners.
* **Festival Way:** Connects the Centre to Ashton Court, great for weekend park rides.

Tip for Visitors: Use high-vis gear if riding at night and stay alert — Bristol drivers are generally courteous, but some streets can be narrow and shared.

Boats & Ferries: Bristol's Floating Transit

One of the city's most charming ways to travel is by boat. Bristol's harbour isn't just pretty — it's practical. The **Bristol Ferry Boats** offer a circular route with multiple hop-on-hop-off stops along the water, making it a fun and efficient way to move between neighborhoods.

Imagine boarding near **SS Great Britain**, gliding past pastel-colored terraces, hopping off at **Castle Park**, and walking right into the Old City — all without touching a single road.

Ferry Tips:
* Operating hours vary slightly by season, with extended routes during festivals and summer weekends.
* You can buy a one-way ticket, a day pass, or even book private tours.
* Ferries are dog-friendly and stroller-accessible.

Trains & Temple Meads Station

Bristol Temple Meads is the main railway station, a stunning piece of Victorian architecture and a vital hub for both local and regional travel. From here, you can connect to:

* **London Paddington** in just 1 hour 30 minutes
* **Bath** in under 15 minutes
* **Cardiff, Exeter, Birmingham, and beyond**

Local services, like the **Severn Beach Line**, offer beautiful journeys along the river and through quiet suburbia — a hidden gem for day-trippers.

Ticket Tip: Use the **GWR app** or **Trainline** to book in advance for better fares. Off-peak and super off-peak tickets offer significant savings.

Taxis, Ubers & Local Rideshares

While not always necessary, taxis can be useful, especially late at night or for early morning airport runs. You'll find black cabs at Temple Meads and in city centre ranks, but booking through apps is more common now.

In 2025, Bristol's rideshare scene has grown to include eco-friendly options like **GreenCab**, an electric-only taxi company. Uber and Bolt also operate in the city, though waiting times can vary depending on time and location.

Safety Tip: Always confirm the license plate and driver's name before getting in.

Accessible Travel in Bristol

Bristol continues to improve its inclusivity across public transport. Most buses and all ferries are wheelchair-accessible, and major stations have lift access.

There are increasing numbers of tactile maps, audio announcements, and hearing loop systems being introduced, especially around Temple Meads, Broadmead, and the Harbourside.

For personalized support, the **Bristol Mobility Centre** offers rental scooters, wheelchairs, and route planning for travelers with additional needs.

When Not to Travel: Managing Peak Times

Bristol's charm lies in its character — but that can also mean congestion during peak hours (8–9:30 AM and 4:30–6 PM). If you're using the bus or planning to drive (not recommended), avoid these windows if possible.

Weekend festivals, especially during summer, also bring road closures and packed public transport. Check the **Bristol City Council's event calendar** for alerts before setting out.

In Bristol, getting around isn't just about function — it's about *feeling* your way through neighborhoods, understanding the rhythm of the streets, and noticing the changes as you move from one community to the next. From the slow pace of a harbourside ferry to the energizing hum of a bicycle ride through Montpelier, every mode of transport offers a new lens on the city.

So take a deep breath, pack a good pair of shoes, and let Bristol carry you gently from one story to the next.

Where to Stay in Bristol

Whether you're waking up to the sound of gulls by the harbor or sipping a morning espresso from a rooftop garden in Clifton, where you stay in Bristol can shape your entire experience. The city is a tapestry of distinct neighborhoods — each with its own tempo, character, and charm — and your choice of accommodation should reflect not just your budget but your travel style.

In this chapter, we'll guide you through the most inviting, well-located, and memorable places to stay in Bristol in 2025. From boutique hotels with riverside views to artistic guest houses tucked into historic quarters, there's something here for every kind of traveler — solo wanderers, families, eco-conscious explorers, and weekend romantics alike.

Let's explore where you'll hang your hat in Bristol.

Clifton: Elegant Charm & Leafy View

Best for: Couples, architecture lovers, tranquil stays

Clifton is one of Bristol's most desirable neighborhoods — and it shows. Home to the iconic **Clifton Suspension Bridge**, Georgian townhouses, and boutique cafés, this area blends old-world sophistication with quiet contemporary cool.

Stay at **The Rodney Hotel**, a charming townhouse that feels more like a cozy manor than a city stay. For something more upscale, **Number 38 Clifton** offers panoramic views, plush interiors, and the kind of breakfast that makes you linger. You'll be within walking distance of **Clifton Village**, brimming with antique shops, delicatessens, and independent bookstores.

Advisory Note: Clifton is hilly and may not be ideal for those with mobility concerns. However, it's very safe, scenic, and just a 15-minute walk from the city centre.

Harbourside: Modern Comfort in the Heart of It All

Best for: First-timers, families, foodies
Bristol's Harbourside is a hub of activity — perfect for those who want to step out of their hotel and be immersed immediately in museums, markets, and waterfront charm. Think **M Shed**, **We The Curious**, and some of the city's best restaurants all just steps away.

The **Bristol Marriott Royal Hotel** offers timeless comfort with views of the harbor and **College Green**, while **Harbour Hotel & Spa** adds a splash of luxury with a subterranean pool and sleek design. If you're traveling as a family, **Premier Inn Bristol City Centre (King Street)** is practical, affordable, and ideally placed between the river and cultural spots.

Local Vibe: Harbourside can be lively into the evening, especially on weekends. If you're a light sleeper, consider asking for a courtyard-facing room or choosing accommodation a few blocks inland.

Stokes Croft & Montpelier: Artsy, Gritty, and Full of Soul

Best for: Creatives, solo travelers, younger crowds

Looking for Bristol's rebellious, artsy spirit? You'll find it in **Stokes Croft** and neighboring **Montpelier**. Murals bloom on every surface, second hand stores spill onto sidewalks, and spoken word poetry nights are more common than pub quizzes.

Stay at **The Full Moon Backpackers**, a social, music-loving hostel with a courtyard bar and festival energy. For a more private option, consider one of the many quirky Airbnbs here — old railway carriages turned lofts, or attic rooms filled with plants and records. **Artist Residence Bristol**, set just south of this area, offers boutique charm inspired by local creatives.

Important Note: This part of town is vibrant but can be noisy and a little rough around the edges. If you're open-minded and enjoy urban energy, it will feel like home. Otherwise, visit during the day and lodge elsewhere.

Old City & City Centre: Central, Convenient & Characterful

Best for: Short stays, nightlife lovers, budget-conscious travelers

The **Old City**, with its medieval street layout and centuries-old pubs, is right at the city's beating heart. It's perfect for visitors who want easy access to everything: shops, bars, museums, and transport hubs.

The **Mercure Bristol Grand Hotel** balances affordability with history, featuring an artistic redesign that pays homage to local street art. For something more contemporary, try **Radisson Blu Bristol** — especially if you love waking up to panoramic harbor views from high above the city.

Safety Tip: Like most city centers, the Old City can get busy and boisterous at night. It's generally safe, but take standard precautions when walking late.

Southville & Bedminster: Local Life on the Rise

Best for: Foodies, market lovers, longer stays

Cross the river and you'll find **Southville** and **Bedminster**, two fast-growing neighborhoods full of indie cafes, yoga studios, and some of Bristol's best street art. This is a favorite with longer-term travelers or digital nomads who want a more "local" experience.

Accommodation here leans more toward short-term rentals and guesthouses. You'll find lovely terrace homes on Airbnb, often with leafy courtyards and retro interiors. Consider booking near **North Street**, which buzzes with restaurants like **Souk Kitchen** and **The Malago**.

Recommendation: If you're in town during the **Upfest Street Art Festival**, staying here puts you right in the creative thick of things — expect painted walls, live music, and spray cans galore.

Eco-Conscious & Quirky Stays

Best for: Green travelers, alternative thinkers

In 2025, Bristol continues to lead the UK in sustainability and slow tourism. If your accommodation priorities include solar panels, upcycled furniture, or permaculture gardens, you're in luck.

Brooks Guesthouse offers stylish "Rooftop Rocket" caravans — think airstream-style trailers perched atop a boutique hotel near St. Nicholas Market. They're fun, photogenic, and centrally located.

Looking for a full eco-retreat? **Beechenhurst Lodge** (a short bus ride away) is a tranquil woodland B\&B that uses rainwater harvesting and organic local food. It's great for a reset after a few busy days of urban exploration.

Luxury Without the Pretension

Best for: Special occasions, romantic getaways

If you're celebrating, treating yourself, or simply enjoy plush robes and crisp linens, Bristol has its share of refined options.

* **Hotel du Vin & Bistro** offers wine tastings and clawfoot tubs inside former 18th-century sugar warehouses.
* **Berkeley Suites** provides fully serviced apartments with artistic touches and high-end amenities.
* For the ultimate harborfront elegance, **Avon Gorge by Hotel du Vin** combines historic architecture with dramatic views of the Clifton Suspension Bridge.

Bristol doesn't just offer beds — it offers **personalities**. The Georgian grace of Clifton, the street-smart creativity of Stokes Croft, the bustling harbor buzz — each area invites a different kind of stay.

Before booking, think about what you want your mornings to feel like. Do you want quiet coffee on a sunny terrace or a buzz of activity outside your window? Do you want to walk out your door into a park, a market, or a museum?

Whatever your travel style, Bristol in 2025 has a corner that feels just right for you.

Eat, Drink & Be Merry

If you want to truly understand Bristol, pull up a chair and start with a fork. This is a city that cooks with conscience and eats with joy. Its food and drink scene in 2025 is a flavorful reflection of everything Bristol stands for — creativity, sustainability, multicultural pride, and a passion for community.

From sizzling street food stalls under historic arches to candlelit tables inside old shipping containers, Bristol is brimming with taste experiences waiting to be savored. Whether you're a plant-based pilgrim, a craft beer aficionado, a spice-chaser, or simply someone who appreciates a good pastry with your coffee, you'll find your tribe (and probably seconds) here.

Let's take a tasty journey through the city's most mouthwatering spots, one bite and sip at a time.

Breakfasts That Make You Want to Wake Up

There's something sacred about breakfast in Bristol. It's not rushed, it's not routine — it's indulgent and imaginative.

Start your morning in **Southville** at **The Farm Café**, where the sourdough is made in-house and the mushrooms are foraged from local woods. Their vegan full English — complete with herby tofu scramble, smoked aubergine, and beetroot hash — is a revelation.

If you're up near **Stokes Croft**, wander into **Elemental**, a minimalist café with maximalist flavors. Their cardamom French toast with blood orange syrup is practically a sunrise on a plate. Coffee? Bristol takes it seriously. Head to **Full Court Press** in the Old City for an education in third-wave brewing — the baristas here speak espresso like it's a native language.

Lunchtime: Markets, Mezze & Midday Magic

At midday, Bristol's energy peaks. Markets hum, windows swing open, and kitchens bloom with smells from every corner of the globe.

No visit would be complete without a lunchtime stroll through **St. Nicholas Market**, the city's oldest and most beloved food market. It's a treasure trove of flavor: Jamaican patties from **Caribbean Wrap**, Ethiopian stews with injera from **Eatchu**, and crispy halloumi wraps that have won cult status.

Craving something lighter? Try **Koocha Mezze Bar** on Zetland Road — a Persian-inspired, fully plant-based eatery where dishes like turmeric cauliflower, vegan kofta, and smoky baba ganoush redefine what "meatless" means.

For river views with your midday meal, head to **Cargo at Wapping Wharf**. These former shipping containers now house some of the city's most exciting kitchens. **BOX-E** offers fine dining in a tiny space with a big heart — their seasonal lunch menus are both beautifully plated and thoughtfully sourced.

Afternoon Indulgence: Cakes, Cider & City Walks

This is Bristol — afternoon snacks are essential. The city's café culture is as comforting as it is creative, and sweet tooths are well looked after.

Stop at **Ahh Toots**, a whimsical bakery tucked beneath the Christmas Steps, where handmade cakes are stacked high with edible flowers and clouds of cream. You'll find everything from pistachio rose loaves to gooey peanut butter brownies. Take your treat to nearby **Castle Park** and watch the boats drift past.

Prefer something savoury with a kick? Grab a cold pint of **Ashton Press cider** and a sharp cheddar slab at **The Apple**, a beloved cider bar housed on a boat. It's here that you'll discover just how deep Bristol's love affair with fermented apples runs.

Dinner Time: Flavour as Philosophy

Dinner in Bristol isn't just a meal — it's often a manifesto. Sustainability, local sourcing, and culinary experimentation are front and center, and every plate tells a story.

For something elegant but unpretentious, try **Wilsons** in Redland. Their zero-waste kitchen turns foraged herbs and homegrown veg into dishes that feel like edible poetry. Menus change daily based on what's available, so no two meals are ever alike.

In Bedminster, **Cor** serves up Mediterranean small plates with bold Bristolian confidence. Think slow-cooked lamb with preserved lemon or charred aubergine with whipped tahini, served in a setting where the vibe is relaxed but refined.

If you're on a budget or simply crave community vibes, **The Thali Café** in Easton is a local institution. Their Indian fusion dishes are served on steel platters, with everything from Goan fish curry to mango dal. Bonus: They use a reusable tiffin takeaway system, making sustainability part of the meal.

Drink Like a Local: Pints, Spirits & Proper Stories

When the sun dips, Bristol comes alive in its pubs, breweries, and hidden speakeasies.

Start your evening with a local pint at **The Grain Barge**, a moored pub with views across the water and beers brewed just up the hill at **Bristol Beer Factory**. Their milk stout is legendary — smooth, rich, and dangerously drinkable.

Craving cocktails? Wander into **Hyde & Co**, a speakeasy-style bar with velvet booths, jazz on vinyl, and a menu full of smoky mezcal, sharp amaro, and curious concoctions. Their bartenders are more like potion-makers than servers.

Prefer a pint with political chatter and an impromptu poetry slam? Head to **The Canteen** in Stokes Croft — where the live music is always free and the drinks menu is full of local lagers and ciders with a social conscience.

Late-Night Bites & Moonlit Munchies

If hunger strikes past 10 PM (and let's be honest, it will), Bristol's late-night scene won't disappoint.

La Panza in Gloucester Road serves late-night empanadas and grilled cheese sandwiches packed with pickled onions, molten cheddar, and herby aioli. For something quick and carby, join the queue at **Taka Taka**, the Greek food spot beloved by night owls, cabbies, and students alike.

Feeling bold? Try the **jalapeño poppers pizza** at **Pizza Workshop** or the vegan shawarma from **Eat a Pitta**. Both spots are open late and generous on the portions.

Seasonal Feasts & Foodie Events
If you're visiting during a festival, come hungry. Bristol knows how to celebrate with food.

* **Bristol Food Connections (June)** brings the whole city together with pop-up kitchens, chef talks, and edible art installations.
* **Upfest** not only decorates walls with world-class graffiti but also lines the streets with global street food trucks.
* **Bristol Craft Beer Festival (September)** is a paradise of small-batch brews and beer-friendly bites.

Farmers markets — like the ones in **Whiteladies Road** and **Tobacco Factory** — also let you taste the region's finest, from Somerset strawberries to West Country cheeses.

In Bristol, eating and drinking isn't just fuel — it's one of the best ways to explore the city's soul. Each dish tells a story. Each pub has a past. Each bite, whether from a tandoor or a tapas plate, connects you with people who live to cook, serve, share, and celebrate.

So take your time. Ask about the ingredients. Say yes to seconds. And remember: in Bristol, flavor isn't just on your plate — it's in the conversations, the music, and the very air.

Cultural Etiquette & Local Manners

When visiting a city as warm and character-rich as Bristol, good manners are more than just polite — they're a passport to genuine connection. Locals here are known for being open-minded, quirky, and full of pride for their city. But like anywhere, there's a unique rhythm to how things are done, and tuning into it can make your visit smoother, deeper, and more enjoyable.

This chapter offers more than surface-level politeness. We'll delve into what makes Bristolians tick — their values, unspoken rules, and social nuances — so you can explore the city not just as a tourist, but as a respectful guest invited into its living, breathing culture.

Greetings & General Courtesies

Let's begin with the basics. In Bristol, as across much of the UK, good manners are foundational. A simple "please," "thank you," and "sorry" — even when you're not at fault — go a long way. Bristolians are friendly, but modest; overt familiarity right away can feel

77

intrusive, so easing into interactions with polite warmth is the norm.

How to Greet People:
* A smile and a quick "Hiya!" or "Alright?" (the Bristolian way of saying "Hello") is common in casual settings.
* In shops or cafes, a friendly "Morning," "Afternoon," or "Evening" is appreciated, especially if you're asking for help or placing an order.

Local Tip: Don't be surprised if someone greets you with, "You alright?" It's not a genuine inquiry into your well-being, but more a Bristolian "hello." A simple "Yeah, you?" works perfectly in return.

Public Spaces & Queueing Culture

If there's one rule you should engrain before stepping onto a Bristol bus or into a local bakery, it's this: **respect the queue**. British people take queuing seriously, and Bristolians are no exception.

Whether it's waiting for the loo at a pub, lining up for jerk chicken at St. Nick's Market, or boarding the Metrobus, always observe the invisible (but sacred) order of arrival.

In public places like **Queen Square**, **Castle Park,** or on the **Harbourside promenade**, noise levels are generally respectful. People enjoy open-air spaces but do so with a kind of understated appreciation — music is kept low, dogs are leashed, and smokers typically step away from groups.

Cultural Insight: Bristolians deeply value shared spaces and have a strong environmental consciousness. Leaving litter behind, especially in green spaces, is a definite faux pas.

Speaking Like a Local: Dialect, Humor & Banter

Bristol has its own distinctive dialect and phrases. You'll likely hear locals refer to children as "babies," use "lush" to describe something wonderful, or sprinkle "cheers" into conversations as a stand-in for thanks or goodbye.

While you're not expected to speak like a local, showing curiosity or affection for the dialect earns you smiles.

Humour in Bristol:
* Sarcasm and irony are common in conversations — it's how Bristolians bond and signal friendship.
* Light teasing, known as "banter," can be affectionate but may be misunderstood if you're unfamiliar. If someone jokingly calls your coat "proper loud," they probably mean it as a compliment in disguise.

When in doubt, take it with a laugh. Bristol is relaxed and open — people here don't take themselves too seriously.

Pub Etiquette & Nightlife Norms

Pubs are cultural institutions in Bristol. They're not just for drinking — they're for talking, reading, eating, debating, or watching the world go by.

If you're heading to a pub like **The Coronation Tap** or **The Old Duke**, here are a few key customs:

* **Ordering:** There's rarely table service. Walk up to the bar, wait your turn (don't shout or wave), and place your order when acknowledged.

* **Rounding:** Among friends, people often take turns buying "rounds." If someone buys you a drink, the polite expectation is to return the favor.
* **Tipping:** Not customary in pubs, though leaving small change is appreciated for exceptional service.

Late-Night Consideration: Bristol's vibrant nightlife means music, dancing, and celebration — especially around **Park Street** or **Stokes Croft**. However, locals value their neighborhoods and sleep! Keep voices down in residential areas after hours and avoid singing on the streets (unless you're at a gig).

Sustainability & Social Awareness

Bristol isn't just proud of its culture — it's **conscientious**. This is a city that was crowned the UK's first **European Green Capital**, and many of its residents walk the talk.

* Recycling is expected; bins are clearly marked, and composting is common in cafés.
* Carry a reusable water bottle or coffee cup. Many cafés, like **Better Food** or **Spicer & Cole**, offer discounts for bringing your own.

* Avoid single-use plastics and say no to bags unless necessary — small but appreciated actions.

Bristol is also known for its activism and progressive values. From supporting LGBTQ+ rights to championing racial equality and climate action, it's a city where inclusivity is not just respected but expected.

Cultural Note: During your visit, you may come across peaceful protests or awareness campaigns. Feel free to engage, listen, or ask questions respectfully — but avoid mocking or trivializing causes that locals care deeply about.

Engaging with Locals: Respectful Curiosity Wins

Bristolians are, by and large, proud of their city and love talking about it — especially over a pint, in a café queue, or while browsing stalls at **Tobacco Factory Market.**

Ask about their favorite street art, local cider, or what they think of the latest installation at **Arnolfini**. Most will respond warmly to genuine curiosity. That said, avoid intrusive questions or controversial topics unless the conversation naturally flows that way.

If you're photographing street performers, buskers, or independent shop fronts, always ask permission — it's a small gesture that goes a long way.

Golden Rule: Be present. Don't treat the city like a checklist — let yourself get swept up in spontaneous chats, music in unexpected places, or a friendly dog who insists on saying hello.

There's no single way to "blend in" in Bristol — and that's part of the charm. The city is proudly individualistic, wonderfully weird, and open to all kinds of people. But kindness, humility, and a willingness to understand the local rhythm will help you leave a positive impression wherever you go.

When you offer up a warm "Cheers," say thank you to the bus driver, wait your turn at the pub, or strike up a conversation with a shopkeeper in **Gloucester Road**, you're doing more than being polite. You're becoming part of Bristol's story — respectfully, meaningfully, and memorably.

Money Matters & Budget Tips

Bristol is not a budget-breaker — not if you know where to look. While this vibrant city is full of boutique shops, award-winning eateries, and upscale accommodation, it's equally a place where you can enjoy world-class culture, rich history, and unforgettable experiences without watching your wallet shrink in panic.

In 2025, Bristol continues to evolve as one of the UK's most value-packed destinations. With a thriving independent scene, walkable neighborhoods, and plenty of free or low-cost attractions, it's a city that rewards the savvy traveler. Whether you're a student adventurer, a solo explorer, or a family stretching your pounds, this chapter is your map to making every Bristol moment count — without overspending.

Let's dive into how to enjoy the best of Bristol, pound for pound.

Understanding Currency & Payment Culture

Bristol, like the rest of the UK, uses the British Pound Sterling (£). In 2025, digital payments have become the norm — tap-to-pay cards, mobile wallets like Apple Pay and Google Pay, and QR code payments are widely accepted, even at small market stalls and street food trucks.

Tips to Keep in Mind:
* **Carry a little cash** for occasional use — some traditional pubs or charity-run pop-ups may still prefer coins and notes.
* ATMs (known as "cashpoints") are widely available, especially near train stations, shopping streets, and convenience stores.
* Check with your home bank about international card fees. Many travelers opt for **travel-friendly bank cards** (like Monzo or Revolut) which offer low or no foreign exchange fees.

Budget-Friendly Accommodation

Good news: Bristol has accommodation to suit all wallet sizes. From waterfront hostels to quirky guesthouses, you can stay central without splashing out.

* **YHA Bristol** – A stylish, centrally located hostel in a converted grain house right on the Harbourside. Great for solo travelers or families who want budget rooms and a communal vibe.
* **Brooks Guesthouse** – A mid-range boutique option offering sleek "Rooftop Rocket" caravans with city views — fun and affordable.
* **Airbnbs in Bedminster or Totterdown** – These neighborhoods are local, colourful, and offer better nightly rates than central hotels — ideal for longer stays or those seeking a homely touch.

Budget Tip: Avoid peak weekends (like during the Bristol Balloon Fiesta or Upfest) unless you book well in advance. Prices surge and budget options disappear quickly.

Eating Well Without Overspending

Bristol is a food lover's dream — and you don't have to dine at fancy restaurants to eat like royalty. The city's multicultural roots and street food obsession mean there are brilliant cheap eats everywhere.

Top Picks Under £10:
* **Eatchu** (St. Nick's Market): Crispy gyoza with handmade dipping sauces. Packed with flavor, light on the wallet.
* **The Athenian** (Wapping Wharf): Greek souvlaki wraps that redefine street food comfort.
* **Eat a Pitta** (Broadmead & St. Nick's): Massive, fresh salads and pittas loaded with hummus, falafel, and pickles.
* **Taka Taka** (City Centre): Beloved by students and late-night wanderers — generous portions and budget-friendly pricing.

Local Insight: Lunch menus often offer the best value. Many mid-range restaurants provide set menus between 12–3pm for a fraction of their evening price.

Transport on a Budget

You don't need a car in Bristol — in fact, it's easier without one. The city is compact, pedestrian-friendly, and full of scenic walking routes.

* **Walking:** Free, healthy, and arguably the best way to explore Bristol's quirky neighborhoods.

* **Cycling:** The **YoBike+ e-bike hire scheme** is affordable and efficient. Just scan and ride — it's cheaper than a taxi and a scenic way to travel.
* **Bus Travel:** Tap your contactless card to board a **First Bus** or **Metrobus**. Fares are capped daily and weekly — making it easy to budget.
* **Boats: Bristol Ferry Boats** offer a unique way to move around the harbor for just a few pounds. Get a day pass and make an afternoon of it.

Smart Tip: Download the **First Bus App** to plan routes and buy discounted e-tickets in advance.

Free & Low-Cost Things to Do

You could easily spend a week in Bristol without paying an entry fee for anything — and still leave feeling full of stories and culture.

Always Free:
* **Bristol Museum & Art Gallery** – From Egyptian mummies to Banksy originals, this hilltop museum is a treasure trove.
* **M Shed** – Located on the Harbourside, it tells the story of the city through the voices of its people.

* **Ashton Court Estate & Leigh Woods** – Acres of green space, ancient trees, deer herds, and views of the Clifton Suspension Bridge.
* **Stokes Croft Street Art Trail** – Just walk and look up. The whole neighborhood is an open-air gallery.
* **Bristol Cathedral & College Green** – Peaceful, historic, and a great spot for people-watching.

Under £10:
* **SS Great Britain** – One of Bristol's most iconic attractions. Entry is under £10 if you book online with a student or child discount.
* **Arnolfini** – Contemporary art gallery on the waterfront, often free exhibitions, or very low-cost events.

Smart Shopping Without Splurging

Bristol's independent shops are irresistible — but you don't have to overspend to bring home something special.

* **St. Nicholas Market** is your go-to for affordable souvenirs: hand-poured candles, artisan soaps, second-hand books, and Bristol-themed art prints.

* **Gloucester Road** is Europe's longest street of independent shops — many offering ethical, upcycled, and budget-friendly treasures.
* For vintage clothing, **BS2 and BS3 postcodes** are treasure chests of bargains — check out **Loot**, **Sobeys**, and **That Thing** for funky finds under £15.

Tip: Avoid shopping in chain-heavy malls like Cabot Circus if you're watching your budget. Prices are higher and items less unique.

Managing Your Money While You Travel

To keep your budget on track, try these simple, empowering habits:

* **Set a Daily Spend Limit:** Use budgeting apps like **Trail Wallet** or **Spendee** to track what you're spending in real time.
* **Buy in Advance:** Book train tickets, attractions, and shows early online for the best rates.
* **Look for Combo Passes:** Some attractions offer multi-entry tickets or family bundles.
* **Ask for Discounts:** Students, seniors, and families often qualify for reduced prices — don't be shy about asking.

Traveling on a budget isn't about limiting your experience — it's about enhancing it. When you spend thoughtfully, you notice more. You seek deeper stories. You discover corner cafés that locals love, walk streets you'd miss in a taxi, and form genuine connections that aren't sold at any price.

Bristol rewards those who explore with intention. With a little planning and the right perspective, you can experience the city's art, food, nature, and community — all without draining your wallet. Empower yourself, pack smart, spend with purpose, and let the city surprise you.

Packing Smart for Bristol

Packing for Bristol in 2025 isn't about stuffing a suitcase—it's about preparing for adventure, layers of charm, and a dash of the unexpected. Bristol is a city that invites spontaneity: one moment you're exploring historic streets in the sunshine, the next you're ducking into an art gallery to escape a sudden shower. The secret to a great visit? Packing smart so you're ready for anything.

Whether you're here for a weekend getaway, a week of exploration, or a longer stay, the key is flexibility. This chapter is your friendly packing companion, guiding you through what to bring, what to leave behind, and how to feel confident, comfortable, and fully prepared for your time in this vibrant, creative city.

The Bristol Weather Puzzle: Layers are Your Best Friend

Bristol's climate in 2025 continues its reputation for being... well, unpredictable. The city enjoys all four seasons, but they often like to share the same day.

Spring (March–May): Expect mild days, cooler evenings, and the occasional drizzle. Trees bloom early in Clifton, and café terraces start to buzz.

Summer (June–August): Pleasant and bright, with average highs around 20–23°C (68–73°F). Sunshine is common, but pack for rain just in case.

Autumn (September–November): Crisp air, beautiful foliage in Ashton Court and Brandon Hill, and cozy pub weather begins. You'll need layers.

Winter (December–February): Chilly, damp, and sometimes windy. Snow is rare, but heavy jackets are a must.

Essentials for Any Season:

* A lightweight, **waterproof jacket** – ideal for spring through autumn.
* **Comfortable walking shoes** – the cobbled streets and hilly neighborhoods (looking at you, Totterdown!) require sturdy soles.
* A compact **travel umbrella** – Bristol showers like to surprise.
* **Layers** – Think T-shirts, jumpers, scarves. You'll thank yourself later.

Everyday Clothing: Blend in, Be Comfortable

Bristolians dress casually, creatively, and comfortably. This is a city where no one side-eyes a vintage tweed jacket, neon Doc Martens, or a thrifted 90s windbreaker. Your wardrobe here should be versatile and you-friendly.

Bring:
* **Jeans or sturdy trousers** – ideal for walking and transitioning from day to evening.
* **Tops in breathable fabrics** – layering is key, so think T-shirts, long-sleeves, and a warm jumper.
* **One nice outfit** – for a special dinner, theatre night at the Old Vic, or cocktails at Hyde & Co.
* **Hat and gloves** – if visiting in late autumn or winter.

Leave:
* High heels and delicate shoes – many streets are uneven, and the city is best explored on foot.
* Excessive dressy outfits – even in fancy restaurants, the vibe is more stylishly relaxed than formal.

Helpful Tip: If you forget something, head to **Gloucester Road** or **Park Street** for independent boutiques, vintage gems, or practical replacements.

Tech & Travel Gear: What to Pack and Power

You'll likely want to document your Bristol experience (it's too photogenic not to), so packing the right tech can enhance your trip without weighing you down.

Recommended Tech Items:
* **Universal UK plug adapter** – the standard is a Type G, 3-pin plug.
* **Portable charger** – from filming the Clifton Suspension Bridge to mapping your next pub, your phone will work hard.
* **Reusable water bottle** – Bristol is proudly eco-conscious, and water refill points are widely available.
* **Headphones** – ideal for solo travelers who enjoy audio walking tours or some personal music in Queen Square.

Insider Tip: Download helpful apps in advance:
* **First Bus App** (for public transport)
* **Visit Bristol** (for events and attractions)

* **Google Maps Offline** (just in case you lose signal)

Health & Safety Essentials: Better Safe than Sorry

While Bristol is generally very safe and traveler-friendly, it's always wise to pack a few items to keep you comfortable and ready for anything.

* **Travel insurance info & copies of key documents** (digital and hard copies)
* **Basic first aid kit** – plasters, paracetamol, antihistamines, and motion sickness tabs for boat rides on the harbor
* **Hand sanitizer** – still a staple in 2025, especially on public transport
* **Prescription medications** – with enough supply and your doctor's note if needed

For Families: If traveling with children, pack extras like sun hats, rain ponchos, snacks, and games or audiobooks for train rides or down time.

What Not to Pack: Trust Bristol to Provide

Let's talk about space-saving. Bristol is a well-equipped, easy-to-navigate city with everything you might need available in local shops or convenience stores like **Boots**, **Co-op**, or **Holland & Barrett.**

Skip packing:
* Heavy guidebooks – this one has you covered!
* Multiple pairs of shoes – one comfortable pair and one evening pair are plenty.
* Hair dryers or bulky electronics – most accommodations include these.

Local Advice: Save luggage room for local goodies — like handmade candles, vintage vinyl, or bottles of Somerset cider. You'll want space for souvenirs.

Sustainable Packing: Travel Light, Tread Lightly

Bristol's environmental ethos runs deep, and visitors are encouraged to respect that by packing with sustainability in mind.

* **Tote bags or reusable shopping bags** – plastic bags are no longer given out freely.
* **Refillable toiletries in solid form** (like shampoo bars or soap bars) to avoid plastic.
* **Notebook or journal** – trust us, you'll want to jot down what you see and feel here.

Feeling generous? Consider packing a few useful items you can donate before you leave — warm gloves, scarves, or books can be left at local charity shops or community shelters.

Packing by Traveler Type: Quick Lists

For the Solo Explorer:
* Travel journal
* Local SIM or roaming plan
* A couple of good books for café breaks

For the Family Traveler:
* Lightweight stroller for hilly streets
* Reusable snack containers
* Extra layers for kids

For the Cultural Connoisseur:
* Outfit for theatre or live music
* Small notepad for exhibitions
* Noise-canceling headphones for museum audio guides

For the Outdoor Adventurer:
* Waterproof daypack
* Trail shoes for Leigh Woods or Ashton Court
* A thermos for long rambles

Packing smart isn't about bringing everything — it's about bringing what matters. When you're prepared, you move through a city with ease, and Bristol rewards that readiness with spontaneity, wonder, and color around every corner.

So pack your curiosity, your comfiest shoes, a raincoat that makes you feel invincible, and a mindset ready for cobbled streets, cider sips, unexpected sunshine, and moments worth remembering.

Here in Bristol, travel isn't about what you carry — it's about what you discover.

Staying Safe & Healthy

Bristol is one of the UK's most welcoming and traveler-friendly cities. Its blend of community warmth, creative energy, and walkable neighborhoods make it a joy to explore. But as with any travel destination, staying healthy and safe is key to making your experience smooth, memorable, and stress-free.

In 2025, Bristol continues to prioritize public wellbeing, sustainability, and accessible healthcare. That said, no trip is immune to a few surprises — a turned ankle on a cobbled street, a forgotten prescription, or simply the discomfort of a new climate. This chapter is your caring companion: a guide to staying well, feeling secure, and navigating the city with the quiet confidence that you're prepared for whatever your journey brings.

General Safety: A City of Kindness with Common Sense

Bristol is generally considered very safe, both day and night. Locals are helpful, public areas are well-lit, and major tourist zones like the Harbourside, Park Street, and Clifton are lively and secure. But like any city, a few precautionary habits go a long way.

Always be mindful of your belongings, especially in busy areas like St. Nicholas Market, Broadmead, or on public transport. Keep your bag zipped, avoid displaying expensive electronics openly, and trust your instincts. If something feels off — a street that's too quiet, someone following too closely — step into a shop or café and reassess.

Avoid isolated areas late at night, particularly near construction zones or unlit pathways along the River Avon. While crime rates are low, opportunistic petty theft can happen.

One of the most reassuring things about Bristol is how often people will help if you're in a bind. Whether it's asking for directions in Bedminster or finding a lost phone near College Green, don't hesitate to speak up — chances are someone will stop to assist.

Emergency Numbers & Where to Go for Help

In an emergency, dial 999 — the UK's universal number for police, ambulance, fire, and rescue. For non-emergencies, you can dial 101 to reach local police or 111 for non-urgent medical advice.

If you need urgent medical care that isn't life-threatening, walk-in centres such as the one at Broadmead Medical Centre can help. For more serious concerns, the Bristol Royal Infirmary (BRI) near the city centre has a 24-hour A\&E department.

It's also worth noting that many pharmacists are qualified to offer health consultations for minor issues — things like headaches, colds, or travel-related stomach troubles. Look for major pharmacy chains like Boots, or smaller independents near Gloucester Road and Whiteladies Road. Pharmacists here are friendly, professional, and happy to help.

Staying Healthy on the Go

Bristol's outdoor lifestyle and farm-to-fork food culture actually work in your favour when it comes to wellness. You'll find organic shops, plant-based cafés, and opportunities for walking and cycling nearly everywhere. But even the healthiest traveler can hit a speed bump — a little fatigue, jet lag, or overindulgence.

Make hydration a priority. Bristol's tap water is clean, safe, and delicious. Carry a refillable water bottle; many public spaces now offer fountains or refill stations, particularly in parks and transit areas.

Eat smart by balancing all the tempting street food and indulgent pub grub with lighter meals — fruit from local markets, vegetarian cafés like Café Kino, or fresh wraps from The Canteen in Stokes Croft.

If you have dietary restrictions, fear not: most restaurants cater to vegan, gluten-free, or allergy-sensitive diets, and staff are typically well-informed. If in doubt, just ask — Bristolians take pride in their inclusive food scene.

A brisk walk through Ashton Court, a gentle bike ride along the harbourside, or a yoga class at Bristol Yoga Centre can help you reset when travel catches up with you.

Mental Wellbeing: Finding Calm in the City

Travel can sometimes feel overwhelming — even when everything is going well. If you're feeling homesick, anxious, or just need a breather, Bristol offers plenty of calming places to pause and reset.

Visit the peaceful Bristol Cathedral for a quiet moment beneath its stained-glass light. Stroll through the Botanical Gardens at the University of Bristol, where plants and silence soothe the soul. Or sit with a cup of tea in a cozy café like Full Court Press or Little Victories and just people-watch.

Bristol has a mindful heartbeat. It's in the community allotments, the open mic poetry nights, and the gentle buzz of markets where conversation and craft matter more than haste. Lean into that. Let yourself move slowly sometimes.

If you're facing more serious emotional struggles, support is available. The Bristol Mindline is a confidential mental health helpline (open evenings) that offers compassionate, non-judgmental listening. You can reach them by dialling 0808 808 0330.

COVID-19 and Post-Pandemic Travel Readiness

In 2025, the UK — and Bristol in particular — continues to maintain hygiene and safety standards shaped by past pandemic lessons. While restrictions have eased, cleanliness and public health are still taken seriously.

Many public venues offer hand sanitizer at the door, contactless entry, and encourage good ventilation. If you're feeling unwell — especially with flu or cold-like symptoms — locals will appreciate it if you wear a mask in enclosed spaces or keep a little extra distance.

Travel insurance that covers illness or changes in plans is highly recommended. While no one wants to cancel a trip, being covered means peace of mind when life happens.

Healthcare Access for Visitors

If you're visiting from abroad, especially from outside the UK, make sure you have travel insurance that covers medical care. While emergency services will treat you if needed, non-urgent care may come with costs if you don't have proper coverage.

Visitors from EU countries can use the GHIC (Global Health Insurance Card), and some reciprocal agreements may apply for countries like Australia or Canada — but always check the most recent policies before you travel.

Many travelers are relieved to find how efficient and kind UK healthcare providers can be — from walk-in centres to GPs. You're not alone if you need help.

Safety While Exploring Nature

Bristol is a city surrounded by natural beauty — rivers, woodlands, rolling hills — and part of its charm is the call to go outside and roam. But outdoor safety matters too.

When hiking around Leigh Woods or exploring the paths above Avon Gorge, wear sturdy footwear and carry water. Trails are generally well-maintained, but weather can change fast, especially near the coast or riverbanks.

Avoid climbing or veering off marked paths, especially around the cliffs near the Clifton Suspension Bridge — the views are stunning, but the drop is real.

If you're exploring at dusk, make sure your phone is charged, and avoid wandering alone in remote areas after dark. Let someone know where you're going, or better yet, take a local walking tour or hike in a group.

Traveling is about wonder — not worry. And the best journeys are made with just enough caution to keep you open to joy and safe from trouble.

Bristol, with its artistic soul, strong community spirit, and easy-to-navigate cityscape, is a place that wants you to feel at home. And when you respect your health, listen to your instincts, and look out for yourself and others, you'll find that Bristol responds in kind — with safety, comfort, and smiles.

Let this chapter be your quiet confidence. You're ready to explore, ready to connect, and ready to do it all with both care and curiosity.

Responsible & Sustainable Travel in Bristol

Sustainable travel isn't just a trend in 2025 — it's a responsibility. And in Bristol, it's a beautifully woven part of the city's identity. As one of the UK's leading green cities and the first to be named European Green Capital back in 2015, Bristol has long been walking the talk when it comes to eco-conscious living. Today, in 2025, the spirit of sustainability has deepened — you'll see it in solar-powered ferries gliding along the River Avon, refill stations dotted across neighborhoods, and community-driven projects inviting visitors to participate in something meaningful.

This chapter is your invitation to explore Bristol in a way that respects its people, nurtures its environment, and connects you to the city beyond the surface. Whether you're here for a weekend or an extended stay, every small choice you make can help ensure Bristol remains vibrant and welcoming for generations to come.

Getting Around, the Greener Way

Start with how you move — because in Bristol, low-impact transport doesn't mean missing out. It means slowing down, noticing more, and embracing the city's rhythm.

Walking is often the best way to experience Bristol. The city centre, Harbourside, Clifton, and Stokes Croft are all pedestrian-friendly. From the moment you step onto Park Street's steep incline or wander through the graffiti-strewn alleyways of Nelson Street, you're part of the local flow.

Cycling is not only encouraged — it's celebrated. With expanded cycle lanes, secure bike parking, and the electric YoBike+ hire scheme, it's easier than ever to rent a ride and zip from the Suspension Bridge to Easton without breaking a sweat. For longer rides, follow the Bristol and Bath Railway Path — a scenic, car-free route connecting two great cities.

Public transport continues to improve its green credentials. The Metrobus fleet now includes hybrid and electric buses, and routes like the M1 and M3 help you cover longer distances quickly and efficiently. Better yet,

Bristol's ferries — a beloved feature of Harbourside life — now include solar-powered options, offering a scenic, sustainable commute between stops like Temple Meads, the SS Great Britain, and Spike Island.

Where You Stay Matters

Choosing responsible accommodation is a powerful way to support the city's values. In 2025, a growing number of hotels, B\& Bs, and hostels in Bristol are going green in meaningful ways — not just token gestures, but structural commitments to sustainability.

Look for lodgings with:

* **Green certifications** like Green Tourism or EarthCheck
* Renewable energy usage and water-saving policies
* Ethical sourcing for bedding and toiletries
* Recycling and composting systems
* Local employment and community engagement

Some great examples include eco-conscious guesthouses in Totterdown, boutique hotels in Clifton using upcycled décor, and hostels near

St. Paul's that run workshops on urban gardening.

If you're using platforms like Airbnb, consider staying in neighborhoods like Southville or Montpelier. These communities embrace slow living and conscious consumerism, making them ideal bases for eco-minded travelers.

Eating Sustainably: From Fork to Field

Bristol's food scene is a powerful reflection of its ethics. Sustainability, locality, and plant-based eating aren't side dishes here — they're central to the culinary identity.

Try **The Cauldron** in St. Werburghs, where meals are cooked over fire using locally sourced ingredients. Or **Root**, which flips the traditional meat-first model by centering vegetables in clever, vibrant ways. For casual bites, **VX Bristol** is a go-to for vegan comfort food, while **Zero Green** on North Street offers package-free snacks and lunches with a conscience.

The **Bristol Farmers' Market**, held on Corn Street every Wednesday, is a fantastic way to buy direct from local producers. Think organic vegetables, sustainable meats, handmade cheeses, and artisan preserves. Plus, you'll meet the people behind the food — always a richer connection than grabbing something pre-packed.

Don't forget your reusable coffee cup. Bristol's cafés — like **Small Street Espresso** and **Spicer+Cole** — often reward customers who bring their own with a discount.

Support Local, Shop Thoughtfully

Sustainable travel isn't just about where you go — it's about what you leave behind and who you support along the way. Bristol is full of independent shops, ethical brands, and artist-run collectives where your pounds do more than buy things — they uplift entire communities.

Skip the chains and head to:

* **Gloucester Road** — one of the UK's longest stretches of independent shops
* **Stokes Croft China** — where beautiful ceramics support community action
* **Bristol Beacon Gift Shop** — offering items from local designers, often made using upcycled or recycled materials

You'll also find refill stations for toiletries, cleaning supplies, and even spices in shops like **Smarter Living**, **Smug**, and **Better Food Co.** Carry a tote bag or two and you'll be ready to browse without single-use plastic guilt.

Connecting with the Community

One of the most rewarding aspects of responsible travel is the human connection. Bristol is not just a city to see, but a city to meet — through its people, its stories, and its activism.

Look out for:

* **Volunteer-friendly community projects** — like urban farms, litter-picking initiatives, or mural-painting days
* **Workshops** — from sustainable fashion at **The Bristol Textile Quarter** to vegan cooking classes
* **Festivals with a conscience** — like **Green Man Bristol**, which focuses on eco-education, live music, and zero-waste initiatives

Bristol's social enterprises are vibrant, often blending art, advocacy, and business in inspiring ways. Spending your money at places like **Coexist Café** or **Bristol Wood**

Recycling Project supports people, not just profits.

Respecting Nature and Public Spaces

Whether you're lounging at Castle Park, cycling along the Avon, or hiking up Brandon Hill for sunset views, practicing care for the environment means leaving every place better than you found it.

Stick to paths in nature reserves. Don't feed the wildlife. Recycle when you can and take your litter with you if no bin's in sight. Even better, pick up any trash you see — it's small, but it speaks volumes.

In Bristol, these choices matter because they echo the city's own green heartbeat — one driven not by perfection, but by intention.

Responsible travel isn't about sacrifice. It's about adding richness, depth, and meaning to your journey. In Bristol, the more consciously you move through its streets, markets, parks, and cafés, the more it opens up to you — with honest conversations, unexpected beauty, and the sense that you're part of something bigger.

You don't need to be perfect. Just a present. Just mindfulness. Just willing to explore in a way that cares for the place, the people, and the future.

This is how we make travel transformative — not just for ourselves, but for the world we step into.

Bristol Month-by-Month

A City That Celebrates All Year Round
In Bristol, the calendar doesn't just tick by—it comes alive. Month after month, this spirited city shifts its rhythm, embracing changing weather, seasonal flavors, and community celebrations that turn everyday corners into stages for creativity, connection, and color. Whether you're drawn to springtime festivals, summer harbor breezes, autumnal foliage, or the warm twinkle of winter markets, Bristol offers something magical in every season.

Planning your visit around a particular month can transform your experience. Maybe you'll catch a balloon-filled sky in August or discover cider-fueled merriment in October. This month-by-month guide captures the essence of the city as it unfolds through the year—full of stories, surprises, and soul.

January: Quiet Charms and a Fresh Start
The holiday glitter may have faded, but January in Bristol has its own gentle glow. The city moves at a slower pace, offering peaceful mornings in cafés, quiet art gallery visits, and

crisp riverside walks wrapped in scarves and mist.

Head to **Brandon Hill Park** for panoramic winter views of the city from Cabot Tower. Explore indoor gems like **Arnolfini** and **MShed**, which often host new-year exhibitions and family-friendly activities. For those chasing deals, the January sales along **Park Street** and **The Galleries** provide retail therapy without the crowds.

February: Fire, Folklore, and Romance

February may be short, but it packs in the warmth with events like **Bristol Light Festival**, illuminating the city with dazzling, interactive installations. It's a visual escape from the darker evenings and a reminder that art belongs outdoors too.

Romantic couples will love the candlelit coziness of places like **The Ox** or a moonlit ferry ride along the harbor. And if you're up for something unexpected, check out **Wassailing** traditions in nearby cider orchards—a centuries-old custom to awaken the apple trees with song, cider, and fire.

March: Green Shoots & Cultural Buzz

Spring nudges its way in, and Bristol begins to shake off its winter layers. Daffodils bloom in **Queen Square**, and the **Bristol Museum & Art Gallery** often debuts new exhibitions. The city buzzes with students returning from winter break, and the energy is contagious.

Catch the **Women of the World Festival** at **Bristol Beacon**, or enjoy an early-spring boat ride as the sun lingers a little longer. March is a fantastic month for those who want a balance between indoor exploration and emerging outdoor adventure.

April: Easter Fun and Blossoming Parks

In April, Bristol blossoms—literally and figuratively. Cherry trees explode in pink near **Victoria Park**, and picnic season begins in earnest.

Families will love **Easter-themed trails** at **Ashton Court Estate** and **Bristol Zoo Project,** while art lovers can enjoy Open Studios in neighborhoods like **St. Andrews** or **Montpelier**, where local creators throw open their doors to the curious.

Don't miss the **St. George's Day events**, often celebrated with a mix of live music, storytelling, and community theatre. And pack an umbrella—April showers are almost guaranteed, but they come with rainbows.

May: Festivals in Full Bloom

By May, Bristol is alive with festivals, outdoor markets, and al fresco everything. This is the city stretching its limbs and showing off.

Start with the **Love Saves The Day** festival—a vibrant celebration of music and creativity in **Eastville Park**. Then stroll through the **Bristol Walk Fest**, which turns the entire city into a pedestrian-friendly playground with guided heritage walks, nature rambles, and themed strolls for all ages.

Pubs spill onto sidewalks, beer gardens hum, and longer evenings set the stage for sunset hangouts at **Clifton Downs**.

June: Sunshine and Street Art

June is a dream month for street culture lovers. The weather is mostly warm, and the skies are a brilliant canvas for the city's many rooftop views.

Explore **Upfest**, Europe's largest live street art festival, which transforms the streets of **Bedminster** into a living gallery. Watch artists create towering murals while live DJs and food trucks turn neighborhoods into festivals.

Music fans will enjoy **Bristol Sounds**, a series of outdoor concerts held against the shimmering backdrop of the Floating Harbour. And it's officially paddleboarding season—hire a board and float beneath the iconic cranes of the Harbourside.

July: Carnival Energy and Open Skies

July delivers peak summer energy. The city is pulsing with life, music, and multicultural vibrance.

The highlight is **St. Paul's Carnival**, a celebration of Afro-Caribbean heritage and one of the UK's largest cultural street parties. Expect steel pan bands, vibrant costumes, sound systems, and an unbeatable community vibe.

Head to **Whitchurch Lane** for fields filled with summer blooms, or catch a film under the stars with one of the city's **open-air cinema nights** in Queen Square or Millennium Square. Sunsets last longer, laughter carries farther, and every evening feels like a celebration.

August: Balloons, Boats & Festival Fever

August in Bristol means one thing: **The Bristol International Balloon Fiesta**. Each year, hundreds of hot air balloons take to the skies from **Ashton Court Estate**, creating a surreal spectacle that draws visitors from all over the world. If you can, catch the "Night Glow" event—a choreographed dance of balloons lit by flame against a night sky.

There's also **Harbour Festival**, a vibrant showcase of music, dance, circus acts, and food stalls that takes over the waterfront. It's Bristol at its most joyful.

Just be prepared for crowds and book accommodation early—this is one of the busiest, most beloved months.

September: Golden Light and Gentle Adventures

As the buzz of summer mellows, September paints Bristol in golden hues. The air cools just enough to make walking pleasurable again, and the city feels like it's exhaling.

Enjoy **Heritage Open Days**, when historical buildings across the city open their doors for free tours and talks. Dive into **Bristol Open Doors**, which gives rare access to places like hidden crypts, behind-the-scenes museums, and secret gardens.

Harvest markets bloom with apples, cider, and fresh-baked goods, and **theatre season** kicks off again at venues like **Bristol Old Vic** and **Tobacco Factory**.

October: Cider, Colour, and Autumn Tales

October wraps Bristol in russet tones and a festive, nostalgic air. It's the perfect month to explore the woods of **Leigh Woods** or crunch through fallen leaves in **Arnos Vale Cemetery**, which often hosts seasonal storytelling or lantern-lit walks.

It's also **cider season**. Visit a traditional cider farm or explore Bristol's many independent cider bars for tastings. And don't miss **Bristol Film Festival**, which hosts screenings in unique venues like cathedrals, museums, and even caves.

As Halloween nears, ghost tours and spooky trails come to life—perfect for families or thrill-seekers.

November: Bonfires and Cultural Warmth

The chill sets in, but November brings warmth in the form of **Bonfire Night** celebrations. Head to **Canford Park** or **Downend** for firework displays and toasty community gatherings.

It's a great month for catching exhibitions, literary events, or an indoor gig at **The Louisiana** or **Rough Trade**. Museums, cafés, and indie cinemas like **Watershed** become cozy refuges.

As Christmas approaches, festive markets begin to appear, and the first signs of winter's magic can be felt in the air.

December: A Bristolian Winter Wonderland

The final month of the year transforms Bristol into a twinkling festive village. The **Bristol Christmas Market** on Broadmead is at full glitter, with handcrafted gifts, mulled wine, and German sausages under glowing wooden chalets.

Head to **Wapping Wharf** for seasonal street food and local artisan pop-ups, or skate beneath the stars at **Millennium Square's ice rink.**

Choirs perform in historic churches, lights drape across the harborside, and every pub seems to glow with fairy lights and laughter.

Whether you're here to shop, sip, or simply wander, December in Bristol is magic written in frost and fairy dust.

No matter when you visit, Bristol is ready with a story. Some months sing with festivals, others hum with quiet charm—but each offers a window into the city's soul. Use this guide to match your travel style with the rhythm of the seasons, and let Bristol reveal itself to you one month, one moment, one memory at a time.

Because the best time to visit Bristol? It's whenever your heart says yes.

Language Tips & Local Lingo

You might arrive in Bristol thinking English is English — simple, right? But the moment someone asks if you're "gert lush" or offers you a "babber," you'll quickly realize that Bristol speaks a language all its own. Don't worry, you're not lost in translation. You're simply stepping into a place where the accent is thick with West Country warmth, and the phrases are packed with personality.

In this chapter, we're going to decode the delightful dialects, slang, and everyday expressions that make up Bristol's linguistic charm. Whether you want to impress a local at the pub, understand what's being shouted from the bus stop, or just have a laugh trying, we've got you covered.

So buckle up, me — you're about to learn the real Bristolian way of chatting.

The Bristol Accent: West Country Meets Urban Cool

First things first: Bristol has one of the most distinct accents in the UK. It's warm, rhythmic, and often features a drawn-out "r" sound — even at the end of words where it doesn't belong. This is called the **Bristol L** — adding an extra "l" to words that end in a vowel. So, "idea" might become "ideal," and "area" could sound like "areal."

You'll also hear "oi" where you expect an "i" — so "time" sounds more like "time," and "right" becomes "roight." The accent is friendly, expressive, and full of life, much like the people who speak it.

And don't be surprised if you hear a bit of Caribbean influence too, especially in neighborhoods like St. Pauls or Easton. Bristol has a proud Afro-Caribbean heritage that has shaped its slang, its food, its music — and yes, its voice.

Bristolian Sayings You'll Want to Know

Here's a quick crash course in some of the most iconic Bristol phrases. Use them wisely, and you might just earn a smile (or a laugh) from a local.

* **"Gert lush"** – Translation: Really great or lovely.
  > **"That pastry was gert lush!"**
  > This is perhaps the most famous Bristol phrase. "Gert" means "very" or "proper," and "lush" is just... well, lush.

* **"Babber"** – Translation: Baby, sweetheart, or friend.
  > **"Alright, babber?"**
  > Used affectionately with friends, kids, or even strangers in a friendly setting.

* **"Cheers drive!"** – Translation: Thank you, bus driver.
  > **Said as you hop off a local bus — it's practically a ritual.**

* **"Where's it to?"** – Translation: Where is it?
  > **"Where's the station to, mate?"**
  > This is a classically Bristolian construction that sounds unusual but is completely standard here.

* **"Proper job"** – Translation: Well done or done properly.
> **"You've done a proper job of that garden."**
> Compliment someone's efforts with this one.

* **"Mind"** – Translation: Honestly, seriously, or a subtle exclamation.
> **"It's cold, mind!"**
> A little flavor word, used at the end of a sentence to emphasize something.

* **"Bristol fashion"** – Translation: Neat, tidy, or done well.
> **"All ship-shape and Bristol fashion."**
> This old nautical phrase comes from Bristol's history as a port city. It's still used with pride.

Getting by with British Slang Basics

Even beyond Bristol-specific lingo, you'll come across everyday British expressions that might leave international visitors scratching their heads. Here's a few to keep in your back pocket:

* **"Loo"** – The toilet.
  > *"Excuse me, where's the loo?"*

* **"Chuffed"** – Pleased or happy.
  > *"I'm well chuffed with my new trainers."*

* **"Knackered"** – Extremely tired.
  > *"After walking up Park Street, I was knackered."*

* **"Queue"** – A line of people. And yes, Brits take queuing seriously.
  > *"There's a queue for that food truck, innit?"*

* **"Innit"** – Short for "isn't it," but used loosely at the end of many sentences.
  > *"That was a good pint, innit?"*

* **"Fiver/Tenner"** – Five-pound or ten-pound note.
  > *"Got a fiver for the bus?"*

These are common enough that you'll hear them everywhere in the UK, but they're right at home in Bristol, often served with a smile and a "ta" (thank you).

Friendly Tips for Language & Conversation

You don't have to master the accent or slang to connect with Bristolians — but showing curiosity and kindness goes a long way. Here are a few tips for chatting like a local:

* **Start with "Alright?"** – It's the classic Bristolian greeting, meaning "Hello, how are you?" But don't overthink it — it doesn't always require an answer.

> **You: "Alright?"**
> **Local: "Yeah, you?"**

* **Don't rush the small talk** – Bristolians appreciate a bit of banter. Whether you're waiting for your coffee or asking for directions, it's not unusual to exchange a few pleasantries. You might even get a weather update along with your latte.

* **Practice, but don't parody** – Locals will laugh *with* you if you try a "gert lush" now and then, but avoid mimicking the accent in a way that feels mocking. It's okay to try — just be genuine.

* **Listen closely in pubs and markets** – Some of the best Bristol banter happens over a pint or a sourdough stall. Listening in (without eavesdropping!) gives you a real flavor for the lingo.

When Words Fail: Body Language Wins

If you're lost in a conversation or misunderstood someone's phrasing, don't worry. Bristolians are friendly and usually quick to explain — or better yet, show you the way. Pointing, gesturing, and a good-natured chuckle are all part of the local communication toolkit.

And if you're ever stuck mid-conversation, you can always fall back on a simple:

> "Sorry, I'm not from round here — what's that mean?"

Chances are, someone will gladly give you a local lesson on the spot.

Language is more than just communication — it's connection. Learning a bit of local lingo helps you go beyond tourist mode and feel like part of the city, even if only for a weekend.

Whether you're trading friendly nods on a bus, chatting with a market vendor, or trying to decipher a pub sign, speaking Bristolian — or at least understanding it — brings you closer to the people who make this city shine.

So don't be shy. Say "alright," raise a glass, and maybe toss in a "cheers drive!" for good measure. You're speaking the language of Bristol now.

For Every Type of Traveler

Every traveler is different. Some chase street art and underground music. Others seek quiet cafés, riverside strolls, or sensory-friendly spaces. Some travel solo, some with kids in tow. And then there are those who plan every second... and those who prefer to follow wherever the vibe leads.

Bristol, at its heart, is a city that welcomes everyone. It doesn't matter if you're here for a weekend of food and fun, a solo soul-searching journey, or a cultural deep-dive — this city flexes to fit your style.

In this chapter, we'll help you find your own version of Bristol. From family-friendly fun to LGBTQ+ favorites, budget picks to luxury splurges, we'll show you how this eclectic city has a little something for everyone.

For the Culture Lover
If your suitcase always includes a museum pass and a notepad, Bristol won't disappoint. The city thrives on creativity — past and present.

Start with **Bristol Museum & Art Gallery**, where dinosaurs, Egyptian mummies, and British masters share space with rotating modern exhibitions. Then make your way to **Arnolfini**, a contemporary art center on the Harbourside that champions boundary-pushing installations, live performance, and critical thought.

Theatre-goers will feel right at home at the historic **Bristol Old Vic**, the oldest continuously working theatre in the English-speaking world. Or, for something edgy and local, try **Tobacco Factory Theatres** in Southville — an intimate venue known for powerful new writing and reimagined classics.

Don't miss **Stokes Croft**, either. It's not a museum — but it is a living gallery. Murals and political street art cover every inch of wall space, creating a dialogue that shifts daily.

For the Family Explorer

Traveling with kids? Bristol makes it easy to keep little ones (and not-so-little ones) engaged, entertained, and occasionally exhausted — in the best way.

The **We The Curious science** center is an absolute must. With hands-on experiments, an indoor planetarium, and rotating STEM exhibits, it sparks curiosity in travelers of all ages. Afterward, hop aboard the SS **Great Britain,** where costumed actors, sound effects, and below-deck scavenger hunts make history feel alive and wonderfully messy.

Need some fresh air? Head to **Ashton Court Estate,** where deer roam free and kite-flying is a weekend ritual. Or explore **Windmill Hill City Farm**, where kids can pet goats, feed chickens, and explore nature play areas in the heart of the city.

Even mealtime is family-friendly in Bristol. Many cafés like **Zaza Bazaar**, **Spicer+Cole**, or **Better Food Co.** offer kids' menus and relaxed vibes — the kind where a little mess or a loud laugh won't turn heads.

For the Budget Traveler

You don't need to splurge to enjoy Bristol. In fact, some of the best experiences here are completely free or cost just a few pounds.

Start with the **Harbourside walk** — a scenic loop past historic ships, colorful houses, and street musicians. Pack a picnic or grab a takeaway falafel from **Eat a Pitta** and find a spot to watch the boats glide by.

Public museums like **MShed** and **Bristol Museum & Art Gallery** are free to enter and packed with local stories. Many neighborhoods also offer self-guided street art walks — just download a map and go Banksy-hunting.

Accommodation-wise, check out **YHA Bristol**, **Full Moon Backpackers**, or affordable Airbnbs in **Easton** or **Totterdown**. And for nightlife, student-heavy areas like **Gloucester Road** offer cheap eats and drink deals almost every night of the week.

For the Solo Traveler

There's something about exploring Bristol alone that feels liberating. Maybe it's the city's walkable scale, or the way strangers here so often become fast friends.

Solo adventurers can wander at their own pace, from **Clifton Suspension Bridge** to **Cabot Tower,** stopping wherever curiosity strikes. The city's many independent cafés — like **Small Street Espresso** or **Full Court Press**

— welcome you in with zero awkwardness and plenty of people-watching.

Solo-friendly activities? Try a pottery class at **Clay Shed**, a storytelling night at **The Wardrobe Theatre**, or a Saturday morning browse at **St. Nicholas Market.**

And when the sun sets, you'll find pubs like **The Bell** or **The Golden Guinea** friendly, casual, and easy to chat your way into a table full of new mates.

For the LGBTQ+ Visitor

Bristol wears its inclusivity proudly. It's home to a vibrant, visible LGBTQ+ community and a growing list of queer-owned businesses and spaces.

The **Bristol Pride Festival**, held every July, is one of the biggest in the UK — a week of parades, drag brunches, live music, and community events that transform the city into a rainbow of celebration.

Day to day, you'll find safe, welcoming vibes in spots like **Old Market Quarter**, home to queer-friendly pubs like **The Queen Shilling**, and inclusive cafés like **Estratti** and **Café Kino**.

Check out **Kiki**, an LGBTQ+ events platform based in Bristol, for up-to-date listings on film nights, socials, and workshops throughout the year.

For the Foodie

If you're the kind of traveler who builds your itinerary around meals, Bristol will keep your tastebuds very, very busy.

Begin with brunch at **Bakers & Co., East Village Café,** or **Pinkmans Bakery** (don't miss the sour-doughnuts). For lunch, the global food stalls at **St. Nick's Market** offers everything from Caribbean jerky to Korean kimchi fries.

Evenings bring the magic. Go bold with small plates at **Root**, refined British cuisine at **Wilson's**, or vegan feasting at **Oowee**. And if you're in town on a weekend, try one of the city's many pop-up food markets — **Harbourside Market, Wapping Wharf,** or **Whiteladies Road**.

Finish with a locally brewed pint (try **Left Handed Giant** or **Wiper and True**) or a cider in **The Apple**, a bar on a boat that's as Bristolian as it gets.

For the Luxury Seeker

Bristol can be rugged and artsy — but it also knows how to pamper. For those wanting a more refined retreat, start with a stay at **Bristol Harbour Hotel & Spa**, **Number 38 Clifton**, or the sleek, design-focused **Artist Residence**.

Explore the high-end boutiques of **Clifton Village**, then book a private hot air balloon flight with **Elite Air**, floating over the Avon Gorge at golden hour. Dine on rooftop terraces at **Bokman**, or enjoy a Michelin-starred evening at **Casamia** (if reservations are available — book early!).

And if relaxation is the goal, book an afternoon at the **Lido Bristol** — a restored Victorian pool and spa offering massages, cocktails, and swims under the open sky.

Bristol doesn't ask you to fit into a mold. It invites you to be curious, be open, and explore it on your own terms. No matter what brings you here — art, adventure, comfort, connection — there's a version of this city waiting just for you.

All that's left to do is find it.

And trust us: whichever path you choose, it's going to be **great**.

Maps, Visual Highlights & Quick Reference

Traveling in a new city can sometimes feel overwhelming, especially one as lively and layered as Bristol. This chapter is designed to be your go-to quick reference — a clear, accessible guide to the city's geography, its must-see spots, and practical tips to keep you oriented and confident as you explore.

Think of this as your visual and informational compass for Bristol 2025. Whether you're planning your day or navigating on the go, these insights will help you make the most of every moment.

Understanding Bristol's Neighborhoods: Where to Go and Why

Bristol's neighborhoods each have a unique personality and charm. Familiarizing yourself with them will help you decide where to spend your time, based on your interests.

* **Harbourside:** The beating heart of Bristol's waterfront, where historic ships, modern bars,

and arts venues like Arnolfini come together. Perfect for a leisurely stroll, a meal with a view, or catching a festival.

* **Clifton:** Known for its Georgian architecture and the iconic Clifton Suspension Bridge, this area offers leafy streets, boutique shops, and some of the city's finest restaurants. A must-visit for stunning views and a touch of elegance.

* **Stokes Croft:** Bristol's creative hotspot, bursting with street art, independent shops, and quirky cafés. Ideal for culture vultures and fans of alternative scenes.

* **Southville & Bedminster:** South Bristol's hubs for foodies and families, with lively markets, parks, and an easygoing vibe.

* **Redland & Cotham:** Residential areas with pretty parks, artisan coffee spots, and a calm pace — great for a relaxed afternoon.

Key Visual Highlights to See and Photograph

When it comes to iconic Bristol sights, some views and places are truly unmissable —

especially if you want to capture the city's spirit in your photos or memories.

* **Clifton Suspension Bridge:** This engineering marvel isn't just a bridge — it's a symbol of Bristol's innovation and beauty. The best spots to photograph it are from the Observatory Hill or the Leigh Woods side at sunset when the light paints the sky in warm hues.

* **Bristol Harbourside at Dawn:** Early risers can enjoy the calm, mirror-like waters reflecting colorful boats and historic warehouses. The soft morning light creates perfect conditions for peaceful photos.

* **Street Art in Stokes Croft:** Each wall here tells a story — vibrant murals, provocative pieces, and Banksy originals (including the famous "Mild Mild West"). Wander slowly, camera ready.

* **The Wills Memorial Building:** This Gothic Revival masterpiece on the University of Bristol campus offers intricate details and a towering spire. Nearby, the greenery of **Royal Fort Gardens** provides a natural counterpoint.

* **Arnos Vale Cemetery:** A Victorian garden cemetery with ornate tombstones, sculptures, and winding paths. Atmospheric and beautiful, especially in soft afternoon light.

Navigational Tips: Getting Around Bristol Efficiently

Bristol is relatively compact but has a mix of hills, waterways, and green spaces that affect how you get around.

* **On Foot:** Walking is often the best way to soak in Bristol's neighborhoods. The city center and Harbourside are particularly pedestrian-friendly. Wear comfortable shoes — some streets like Park Street and parts of Clifton can be quite steep.

* **By Bike:** Bristol is one of the UK's most bike-friendly cities. You'll find plenty of dedicated cycle lanes and rental options, such as **YoBike** or **Bristol Bike Share.** Cycling along the harborside or through **Ashton Court Estate** is both scenic and practical.

* **Public Transport:** The city has a network of buses operated mainly by **First Bus** and **Stagecoach**. Key routes connect the city center with neighborhoods like Bedminster,

Easton, and the airport. Buy a **day saver ticket** for unlimited travel and check real-time apps to avoid waiting.

* **Ferries and Water Taxis:** For a scenic twist, use the **Bristol Ferry Boats** on the Floating Harbour. They connect the city center with hotspots like Bristol Zoo, M Shed, and SS Great Britain, all while offering lovely views from the water.

* **Taxi and Ride-Sharing:** Black cabs are available, but app-based services like **Uber** and **Bolt** are often more affordable and reliable for tourists.

Quick Reference Essentials

Here's a handy list of quick facts and contacts to keep in your travel arsenal:

* **Emergency Services:** Dial 999 for police, fire, or ambulance.

* **Tourist Information Centre:** Located at Bristol Temple Meads Station and the Harbourside. Friendly staff can help with maps, event info, and bookings.

* **Wi-Fi Hotspots:** Free Wi-Fi is available in the city center, libraries, and many cafés.

* **Currency Exchange & ATMs:** Widely available in the city center, especially around Cabot Circus and Broadmead.

* **Language:** English is the main language, but Bristol's diverse communities mean you'll hear many tongues around town.

* **Local Weather:** Known for its changeable weather, always carry a light raincoat or umbrella, even on sunny days.

* **Public Restrooms:** Facilities are available at main parks, museums, and shopping centers like Cabot Circus.

Visualizing Your Day: Sample Walks

To help you get started, here are a couple of simple routes designed for maximum impact and ease:

Harbourside Loop (Approx. 2 hours)

Start at **Bristol Cathedral**, walk down to **M Shed,** then follow the water past **Arnolfini, We The Curious,** and the **SS Great Britain.**

End at **Wapping Wharf** for coffee or a bite. This route showcases history, art, and modern life in one tidy package.

Clifton & Suspension Bridge (Approx. 3 hours)

Begin at the **Clifton Village** café strip, wander through **Clifton Down**, and cross the **Suspension Bridge** on foot. Head down to Leigh **Woods** for a nature break before returning by bus or bike. Perfect for a blend of urban charm and green escape.

Helpful Visual Tools

When you're out and about, consider using:

* **Offline Maps Apps:** Download apps like **Maps.me** or **Citymapper** before your trip. They save data and provide accurate routes without cell coverage.

* **Photo Spots Guide:** Ask locals or your accommodation for insider tips on lesser-known viewpoints. Bristol is full of hidden gems beyond the main postcard scenes.

* **Event Boards and Social Media:** Check community noticeboards in cafés or local Facebook groups for pop-up markets, street fairs, or last-minute performances.

Bristol in 2025 is a city that invites discovery and rewards curiosity. With this chapter as your foundation — from clear neighborhood breakdowns and iconic photo spots to practical travel tips — you'll move through the city with ease and confidence.

Maps and guides can only go so far, though. The real magic happens when you pause to look up, talk to a local, or follow a narrow lane that leads to a cozy café or a hidden mural.

So take this chapter with you, but don't forget to wander freely. Bristol is as much about finding unexpected moments as it is about ticking off must-see sights.

Happy exploring!

Final Notes, Challenges & Memories

Every trip leaves its imprint, a mosaic of moments that linger long after the suitcases are unpacked and the postcards put away. Bristol is no different — its streets, stories, and spirit have a way of embedding themselves in your heart. But travel isn't always seamless, and every adventure carries with it small hurdles, unexpected lessons, and unique memories that shape how you see the city and yourself.

As you wrap up your Bristol journey, this chapter offers space to reflect on what you've experienced, what challenges you might have faced, and how you can carry the magic of Bristol forward. Whether this was your first visit or your fifth, Bristol has a way of surprising you again and again.

Embracing Bristol's Complexity

Bristol is a city of contrasts and layers — historic yet cutting-edge, rough-edged yet nurturing, bustling yet peaceful. It wears its history proudly, from its maritime heritage and role in the transatlantic trade to its reputation as a contemporary cultural hub. This mix sometimes means visitors encounter places or situations that don't fit the polished postcard image.

In 2025, Bristol continues to grow and evolve, grappling with urban challenges like housing affordability, sustainable development, and social equity. You might notice pockets where regeneration meets gentrification, or hear conversations that echo the city's ongoing journey toward inclusivity and environmental stewardship.

These realities enrich your visit by reminding you that Bristol is not a static backdrop — it's a living, breathing community striving for a better future. Your respectful curiosity and open heart can deepen your connection to the city beyond sightseeing.

Common Travel Challenges—and How to Handle Them

No trip is without its little hiccups. Here are some of the more common challenges visitors face in Bristol — and some tips to turn them into opportunities.

* **Weather Surprises:** Bristol's famously changeable weather can catch visitors off

guard. Even in summer, a sudden drizzle or gusty wind is par for the course. The best approach? Dress in layers, carry a compact umbrella, and be flexible with outdoor plans. When the rain arrives, take shelter in a cozy café or visit one of Bristol's many museums.

* **Navigating Hills:** Bristol's topography is charming but hilly. Some streets, like Park Street or parts of Clifton, demand stamina. Pace yourself, use public transport or bikes when needed, and don't hesitate to take breaks. The stunning views from the hilltops make every step worth it.

* **Crowds and Peak Times:** Popular areas such as the Harbourside and Clifton can get busy, especially during festivals or weekends. To avoid feeling overwhelmed, try early mornings or weekday visits. Explore lesser-known neighborhoods like Totterdown or Redland for a more relaxed vibe.

* **Finding Local Gems:** With Bristol's rich cultural tapestry, it's easy to stick to the familiar and miss hidden gems. Use local blogs, ask shopkeepers or baristas for recommendations, and allow time to wander

without a strict itinerary. Some of Bristol's best memories come from unplanned detours.

* **Getting Around:** While Bristol's public transport network is decent, occasional delays and limited night services can be a challenge. Plan ahead, keep transport apps handy, and consider walking or cycling for short distances.

Stories from the Streets: Memorable Moments

Travel is as much about people as places. The stories you collect from the city's residents, fellow travelers, and even brief encounters are what make your visit truly unique.

Maybe it was the barista at Small Street Espresso who insisted you try a Bristol cream tea, or the local artist in Stokes Croft who shared the story behind a striking mural. Perhaps a spontaneous chat at a market stall introduced you to a new kind of cheese or a hidden café. Or a ride on the ferry across the Floating Harbour gives you a fresh perspective on the city's waterfront, accompanied by the laughter of families and friends.

For many, the warmth of Bristol's people — their friendliness, humor, and resilience — is what makes the city unforgettable. Even brief moments of kindness, a shared smile, or a helping hand can transform a trip into a cherished memory.

Leaving with Lessons and Inspiration

When you leave Bristol, you take more than souvenirs. You carry lessons about community, creativity, and sustainability. You've seen how a city honors its past while innovating for the future. You've witnessed how street art can be a powerful voice for change, how food can tell stories of migration and culture, and how green spaces nourish urban souls.

Bristol encourages reflection — on how we live, connect, and care for our shared world. Whether it's through a visit to a community garden, participation in a local festival, or conversations with locals, the city invites travelers to think beyond themselves.

Tips for Keeping the Bristol Spirit Alive

Back home, it's easy for travel memories to fade. Here are some ideas to keep the spirit of Bristol with you long after your visit:

* **Create a Travel Journal or Blog:** Write about your favorite spots, the people you met, and the food that surprised you. Include photos or sketches for a personal touch.

* **Cook Bristol-Inspired Meals:** Try making a dish you loved in the city — maybe a vegan feast from a local restaurant or a classic cream tea.

* **Support Bristol's Artists and Causes:** Many artists have online shops, and Bristol-based nonprofits welcome international supporters. Staying connected to the city's creative and social heart helps sustain its vitality.

* **Plan Your Next Visit:** Bristol is a city that rewards return visits. Each season brings new festivals, exhibitions, and experiences. Start a mental or physical list of what you want to explore next time.

Final Reflections: The Journey Continues

Traveling to Bristol in 2025 means more than seeing landmarks; it's about stepping into a vibrant cityscape alive with history, art, community, and challenges. It's about embracing both its polished streets and its unfinished stories.

Your trip may have come to an end, but your relationship with Bristol is just beginning. The memories you made, the lessons you learned, and the connections you felt are seeds planted for a lifelong appreciation.

As you close this guidebook and open the door back to your daily world, carry Bristol with you — its color, its spirit, and its enduring promise of creativity and change.

Until next time, take care, and keep Bristol's heartbeat close.

Safe travels and heartfelt thanks for choosing to discover Bristol.